DIANA

Remembering the Princess

Inspector Ken Wharfe, MVO, was personal protection officer to the late Diana, Princess of Wales, in charge of round-the-clock security at home and abroad, from 1987 until 1993. His memoir, *Diana: Closely Guarded Secret*, was a bestseller on its first publication, and again when it was reissued in a revised edition in 2016.

Ros Coward is a writer and journalist, and the author of a number of well-received books on subjects ranging from feminism to environmental issues. She was chosen by the Diana, Princess of Wales Memorial Fund and the estate to write *Diana: The Portrait*, published in 2004, a book which was based on over 400 interviews with those who knew Diana well.

DIANA

Remembering the Princess

Reflections on her life twenty-five years on

Inspector Ken Wharfe MVO and Ros Coward
with Linda Watson-Brown

jb

First published in the UK by John Blake Publishing
an imprint of Bonnier Books UK
4th Floor, Victoria House
Bloomsbury Square
London WC1B 4DA
England

Owned by Bonnier Books
Sveavägen 56, Stockholm, Sweden

www.facebook.com/johnblakebooks
twitter.com/jblakebooks

First published in hardback and paperback in 2022

Hardback ISBN: 978-1-78946-636-2
Paperback ISBN: 978-1-78946-665-2
Trade paperback: 978-1-78946-635-5
Ebook ISBN: 978-1-78946-637-9
Audiobook ISBN: 978-1-78946-640-9

British Library Cataloguing-in-Publication Data:
A CIP catalogue record for this book is available from the British Library.

Design by www.envydesign.co.uk

Printed and bound in Great Britain by Clays Ltd, Elcograf S.p.A

1 3 5 7 9 10 8 6 4 2

Text copyright © Ken Wharfe and Ros Coward 2022

John Blake Publishing is an imprint of Bonnier Books UK
www.bonnierbooks.co.uk

'Everyone needs to be valued. Everyone has the potential
to give something back.'
DIANA, PRINCESS OF WALES (1961–97)

CONTENTS

INTRODUCTION/
TIMELINE

DIANA WAS BORN on 1 July 1961, the third daughter of John Spencer, Viscount Althorp, and his wife Frances. Park House, where she spent her early years, was on the royal Sandringham Estate in Norfolk and rented from the Queen. When Diana was six, her parents separated and divorced two years later. Her mother married Peter Shand Kydd, heir to a fortune made from wallpaper manufacturing and who for a while was living in Australia as a sheep farmer. In 1975, Diana became Lady Diana Spencer when her grandfather died and her father succeeded to his title as the eighth Earl Spencer. The family then moved to the family seat, Althorp House in Northamptonshire. Diana and her younger brother, Charles, initially went to live with their mother in London but in a bitter battle in which her own mother testified against her, Frances lost custody of her children to her husband. Charles and Diana returned to live at Althorp and in 1976 Earl Spencer married Raine, Countess of Dartmouth, who was also daughter of the romantic novelist, Dame Barbara Cartland. All the Spencer children disliked her intensely and called her 'acid Raine'.

Diana went to West Heath Girls' School in Kent but was not academic and followed a typical English upper-class route of leaving early and attending a finishing school in Switzerland for a year before beginning work at a London kindergarten. Her older sister, Sarah, had previously been romantically linked with the Prince of Wales, but it was Diana who became engaged to Charles in 1981 when she was only nineteen years old. After an exceptionally brief courtship, Diana then moved to Clarence House, the home of the Queen Mother, where she lived until her marriage on 29 July 1981 at St Paul's Cathedral. The wedding was watched by 750 million people across the globe and represented a highpoint in the popularity of the British monarchy. The couple honeymooned in Gibraltar, followed by a cruise through the Mediterranean. On 21 June 1982, their son, William, was born, to be followed on 15 September 1984, by their second son, Harry.

After Harry's birth, Diana began making solo royal trips abroad and, in a visit to the White House in Washington DC, was pictured dancing with John Travolta and Clint Eastwood. Trips to Canada, Japan, China and Australia followed, with media interest gaining even more traction. In 1987, Diana visited Middlesex Hospital, London, where she first shook hands with an AIDS patient. Palace advisors had initially tried to dissuade her from doing so, but she was determined to break the stigma which surrounded the condition at the time.

Her international trips continued, as did her humanitarian work, but Diana's private life was unravelling. The Prince of Wales was continuing his relationship with Camilla Parker Bowles, a liaison which many of their friends colluded with, leading to Diana feeling ostracised and betrayed. Her work with those suffering from HIV/AIDS, cancer and leprosy increased, and she continued to work with many other charities.

In 1992, a sensational book was published by the journalist, Andrew Morton – *Diana, Her True Story* – which was based on tape-recordings made by Diana and given to him in secret. The book laid bare her life with Charles and the troubles she faced in her royal role. In November of that year, Diana and Charles took their last trip together abroad. The following month, the Prime Minister, John Major, announced the official separation of Charles and Diana. During the ensuing year, Diana continued her charity and humanitarian work, visiting Red Cross relief projects including the site in Nepal of the Pakistani International Airline plane crash, and also the refugee camp at Tongorara in Zimbabwe, where her caring side was more obvious than ever. Soon after these trips, she pleaded for 'some time and space' after thirteen years in the spotlight. She cut down her number of official engagements, but after a lengthy break did continue to do more work for the charities she supported. In 1994, she was named International Humanitarian of the Year in the USA. In June of that year, Prince Charles admitted his infidelity with Camilla in a TV interview with Jonathan Dimbleby. That same night, Diana attended dinner at the Serpentine Gallery dressed in a beautiful off-the-shoulder black silk evening gown. The gown was designed by Christina Stambolian and resulted in one of the most instantly definable images of

Diana's life as a royal figure. In November 1995, Diana appeared in the infamous Martin Bashir *Panorama* interview, in which she made her memorable comment, 'There were three of us in this marriage so it was a bit crowded.'

In August 1996, her marriage to Charles was dissolved with the granting of a decree absolute.

In July 1997, Diana carried out her last official engagement at the Children's Unit of Northwick Park and St Mark's Hospital in Harrow, north-west London.

The following month, on 31 August 1997, Diana and Dodi Fayed were killed in a car crash in Paris; their driver also died, and their bodyguard was terribly injured. Diana's funeral was held on 6 September at Westminster Abbey, followed by her burial on an island in the lake at Althorp.

CHAPTER 1

KEN WHARFE

*'I'm sorry, Ken, I'm going through
a very difficult time.'*

THE LONG AND the short of it is that I was Diana, Princess of Wales's personal protection officer for almost six years and, as such, had a unique position as someone who saw behind the veil of the royal world, standing alongside the most charismatic member of that family who has ever lived.

Initially, in November 1986, I was brought in to guard her sons, the Princes William and Harry, and then the Princess herself the following year. From then until November 1993, when I resigned, my job was to protect and guard the most famous woman in the world. During this time, when her image was known to virtually everyone, when she graced the covers of magazines and newspapers ensuring that their sales would soar, and when she toured the world followed by an ever-growing coterie of journalists and photographers, I was the one ensuring her safety.

I was also her friend.

The way her life would end would never have crossed my mind during the years she confided in me about her life and marriage. My position afforded me some quite incredible experiences, and I genuinely enjoyed being with Diana and her boys. But things change – and by November 1993, I had realised two things: that I was unhappy in my role, and that I felt Diana was compromising her own security with her behaviour and misplaced beliefs in the motives of those around her. I actually believed that she wanted me to quit, but found herself unable to bring this about.

'With great reluctance but in the best interests of us both, I have decided to resign as your personal protection officer, Ma'am,' I told her as we arrived back at Kensington Palace one day. 'I'll ask to be assigned to other duties within Royalty Protection as soon as possible.'

My voice seemed rather cold to me, even though I was the one speaking the words, and perhaps that is why Diana said nothing in reply. She exited the car and walked into the Palace – never once looking back. Chief Superintendent Colin Trimming, the Prince of Wales's principal police officer who was my team leader, believed that things would pass over between Diana and me. But I disagreed and requested that he respected my decision.

Within a couple of days, the news hit the press. One paper led with the headline 'Diana Loses Her Top Cop' and I must say that the media treated my resignation with absolute fairness. I had worked alongside these journalists for many years, often securing them access to the Princess against all odds, and they – quite rightly – saw my departure as something of a watershed moment. They seemed to agree that she had not only lost someone who always put her safety first and foremost, but also one of her few true friends.

I didn't engage with the media and I was soon given a new role in charge of security for visiting foreign royalty and VIPs. It was a weight off my shoulders to have left the Palace and I was in no doubt that I'd done the right thing.

A few days later, her Private Secretary, Patrick Jephson – who remains to this day a close personal friend of mine – called and said to me, 'The Princess is insisting that you see her at Kensington Palace – You've got to go back, Ken, she wants to see you.'

'Okay, fine,' I said. 'I will, of course.'

Within days, Patrick had set up the meeting.

It hadn't been a particularly pleasant parting with Diana, but I was perfectly happy to meet with her and see what she had to say. However, I didn't want to have one of her ubiquitous personalised carriage clocks handed over to me, and very much hoped that wasn't what I was being called in for. We'd had a great relationship for so long and it had been rather unpleasant to see it finish the way it did, but I held no hard feelings. I knew that I'd acted in good faith and had never been one of the people Diana felt were against her; I most certainly hadn't been part of any spying on her that she may have felt was going on, no matter her allegations.

Three weeks later, I was at Kensington Palace and it was like the day I first met her at Sandringham House in the mid-1980s. She was the Diana I remembered – fun, laughing and extremely engaging. We sat on the sofa and had a cup of tea.

'First of all, I apologise for my behaviour, Ken,' she began. 'I'm going through a very difficult time and life for me is becoming even more difficult.'

'That's okay, I understand it happens to all of us, Ma'am – but it's good to see you again.'

As we sat in her drawing room drinking tea, laughter soon dominated the discussion. We were reminiscing about the fun of both public and private engagements that we had shared over the past six years. Finally, she said:

'I just wanted to see you and say sincerely thank you so much for all you've done, for me and my children. We've had some good times, haven't we? We've laughed a lot. You've been very good to me, Ken, you've given me a lot of decent advice. If you could, what would be the one piece of advice you'd give me now?'

'Goodness,' I thought. I'd never been asked so directly to give my take on things to a member of the Royal Family before! I thought very carefully but was on the spot. Eventually I responded. 'The only piece of advice I would give is this – Scotland Yard have been with you now for almost twelve years. It's not been easy for you, we have been an invasion of your privacy and I suspect that's why this is beginning to happen. But look, we did give you some privacy, think of the fun times we had where we made it work. My only advice therefore is, whatever you do with your life, you'll always be Diana, the Princess of Wales. You can change your name, you can change your hair, you can have a sex change if you like' – there was much laughter at this – 'but people will still know who you are. For that reason, your security needs will in my view become even greater, and for this reason what you have enjoyed from the beginning is the best the country can offer – so please retain your Scotland Yard security. We know how you work.'

Diana nodded and said, 'You're right, Ken, you're right.' With that, she handed one of the blessed carriage clocks over to me.

It was a pleasant enough meeting and I wasn't one for bitterness, certainly not in this situation, which had ended in a rather inevitable way. The renowned columnist Lynda Lee-Potter of the *Daily Mail* soon wrote a piece looking at what the parting would mean to Diana:

> 'The departure of her personal bodyguard, Detective Inspector Ken Wharfe, was cataclysmic because he was loyal, shrewd, respectful, good fun and above all full of common sense. He more than anybody kept her in touch with reality and the truth.'

I appreciated those words, but I also knew that Diana, with her tendency to read everything written about her, would be faced with them too.

In January 1994, six weeks after we parted, Diana abandoned her security detail completely. Two months after that, I had just returned from the Belgian Embassy in Belgrave Square, London, having been organising security for a forthcoming visit by a member of the Belgian royal family. I was walking through a mews off Belgrave Square with a colleague when a black Audi stopped beside me. Diana was driving it.

'Hey, Ma'am. What are you doing here?' I exclaimed.

'Look behind me,' she said.

There were two photographers following her on scooters, now photographing our conversations. 'This is exactly what I was talking about. Do you want me to come with you?' I asked.

'No, no, you don't need to do that,' Diana replied. 'I have to learn to deal with this.'

'It's best that you drive off. I'll do what I can to delay your unwelcome escort – good luck,' I replied, waving to her as she pulled out and disappeared into traffic.

Next day, the *Sun* proclaimed, 'Di's Secret Meeting With Cop Pal – Chat in Quiet Lane'. They went on to say that this meeting had been arranged and that Diana wanted to talk to me about the 'fact' that I had been forced out by courtiers who were against her. Since this was completely untrue, I made the decision to sue.

When my action came to light, Diana wrote a furious letter to me – she felt that she should have been consulted before I decided to take legal action (which had actually been done after I had contacted the Police Federation, who instructed solicitors on my behalf). She was clearly concerned that she might face a subpoena, which would force her to give evidence, and as a result she had overreacted quite considerably. She need not have worried – the *Sun* settled out of court, given that they knew their story was completely fabricated.

That impromptu meeting in Belgrave Square was the last time I saw her.

In August 1997, I was renovating a property in Dorset, restless and unable to sleep. There was no house telephone, and mobile phones were not a constant presence in those days; however, I did have a pager. At around 4 a.m., the vibration of the pager dancing on the bare wooden floor broke through my slumber. The message urged me to contact Chief Superintendent Dai Davies of the Royalty and Diplomatic Protection Department of the Metropolitan Police. I quickly threw on some clothes and went to the local telephone box alongside the village church.

I was put through to him and, without any preamble to what he was about to say, he told me, 'I'm afraid I have some very bad news for you, Ken.'

'I didn't expect it to be good at this time of the morning,' I replied jovially.

'Ken, I regret to tell you that the Princess of Wales was killed in a road accident in Paris a few hours ago. I'd like you to return to London as soon as possible to help coordinate the funeral arrangements.'

Naturally I agreed, albeit in something of a daze. I walked back to my cottage with those shocking words running through my mind.

Diana was dead.

CHAPTER 2

ROS COWARD

'They need to get rid of me.'

OVER NINE MONTHS in 2003, I conducted nearly two hundred interviews for my book on Diana, which had been commissioned by the Diana, Princess of Wales Memorial Fund. At that time, we already knew that hers would be a lasting legacy, but twenty-five years after her death, it is clear that it's also a contested one.

When anyone of high profile in the public eye dies, obituaries pour in, and everyone learns something they perhaps didn't know – but then interest and discussion normally die down. Usually there is pretty much a consensus about what the person's life consisted of and agreement that there is little more to say. In Diana's case, though, that hasn't happened. Instead, the interest has grown. Not only are there books, films and TV programmes still being produced, but there is little accord between them; they all still seem to ask, however, *who was she really?* It is strange that there are still questions about who the real Diana was and questions about whether she was a good person or a bad person. Was she really the compassionate woman whose charitable work and the caring way she approached people touched the hearts of millions? Or was there something else to her character? Was she perhaps paranoid or manipulative?

People still ask – which parts of Diana can we know, can we *trust* that we know, and which parts remain shrouded in secrecy? Quite rightly, there were parts of her life the public were not aware of – she deserved some degree of privacy after all, especially as she gave so much of herself to the public. But in the last period of her life, so many tantalising elements connected to her life have emerged that, far from settling down into an agreed view about who Diana was, the evidence is still being dug over. There continues to be a sense that there may still be other things to learn. Who knows what may still be released into the public sphere either by people who have never spoken out before, or from records and personal items which have not yet been revealed?

The fact that Diana died so early, so dramatically and in such unexpected circumstances in a completely left-of-centre accident was shocking enough, bringing with it much speculation about the precise circumstances of the accident. But what has added to the continuing interest in her death were the remarks she had previously made. In her anxiety, at certain stages of her life, Diana was said to have made comments such as, *They need to get rid of me*, and *They'd like it if I wasn't around.* Such quotations have fuelled notions that she predicted her own demise, or even that she correctly suspected she was at risk. Those forecasts and statements mean that the accident will inevitably be looked at and revisited endlessly. That a British Royal, a Princess, the wife to the future King, could come out with such astonishing observations about how she believed her own life could end is extraordinary – and those people prone to conspiracy theories who very passionately took her side and felt she had been unfairly treated, no doubt feel that they will always have strong grounds for thinking her predictions were based on reality.

Even though I'm convinced Diana's death was an accident – if you were going to organise an assassination, it would be far too unpredictable to do it through such a staged event – it is typical of the contested memory of Diana. People still speculate on what did actually happen in that Paris tunnel? Who was the woman who died in it? What was actually happening in her life towards the end? Was she really in a serious relationship with Dodi Fayed? Or was he a convenient distraction?

At the time of her death Diana had become a pretty assured, confident woman able to operate on the world stage. Tony Blair, who became Prime Minister in May 1997, had discussed an ambassadorial role with her. The summer before she died, she had travelled to Bosnia and Angola where she had fronted the work of charities involved in removing mines from former war zones. They were typical of the direction she was travelling in, towards difficult and high-profile work. Yet, sadly, it seems that in terms of feeling secure within relationships, even at the end, she was still looking for something that would give her that security. From accounts like the well-researched book *Diana: Her Last Love* by Kate Snell, which have emerged since Diana's death, it appears that she had found it with Hasnat Khan, the heart surgeon whom she had fallen desperately in love with. He appears to have been a decent man who just couldn't cope with the celebrity circus

Diana brought. Then, as the world knows, after Khan backed off, she bounced into an apparently comforting relationship with Dodi Fayed, the man who died with her that fateful night in Paris. Those relationships and what they would have meant for the future in Diana's life have left plenty of unanswered questions that add to the mystery of Diana.

It isn't just the mystery of her death and the unknown elements of her private life that seem to leave much to be explored, there is also the sense of lost promise. When I researched my previous book, I often heard that Diana was quite savvy about how the Royal Family should move into the twenty-first century – many interviewees commented on her instinctive grasp of the fact that the Royal Family needed to work harder to win popularity and the consent they needed to rule. Diana of course had a great deal to contribute to that popularity and the Royal Family could have benefited enormously from her wisdom on this subject. All of that was lost when she died. All of it was wiped out, leaving the question of what might have been to biographers and historians.

Diana's death and the way in which she was lost to the world is merely one layer of what continues to intrigue us. Her life – the slow saga of her marital disintegration and divorce – and her subsequent death exposed to the public many negative things about the Royal Family, and about Prince Charles in particular. The way Diana presented herself and her level of popularity not only exasperated and tainted the monarchy while she was alive, but in the years afterwards and time since. In the period leading up to her funeral and at the funeral itself, the atmosphere throughout the country was almost febrile – people were devastated, they turned up to Kensington Palace and Buckingham Palace to lay flowers, they wandered around weeping, the TV schedules were given over almost entirely to Diana, avalanches of letters were written to her, people waited for eight hours to sign books of condolence. Many people were lost, many were distressed – but they were also angry that the Royal Family didn't appear to care, that they had sealed themselves away in Balmoral with nothing seen or heard of them. There was no personal statement from the Queen; there were no gestures of loss or emotion. The gulf between them and their subject had never seemed wider.

In the days after her death and while the crowds continued to pour into London to lay flowers at the gate of Kensington Palace, the *Daily Express* ran a headline aimed at the Queen, which simply said, 'Show Us You Care, Ma'am'. It summed up a widespread feeling that the Royal Family were indifferent to Diana's fate and therefore complicit in her unhappiness. The editorial calling on the Queen to acknowledge the esteem in which Diana was held did seem to produce the result of the royal flag being lowered to half-mast at Buckingham Palace, but many wondered how genuine the gesture was.

Finally, on 5 September, the Queen spoke to the nation from Buckingham Palace. The speech gives insight into how the Royals finally addressed the life and loss of the rogue Princess, and gives a fair and generous assessment of a woman whom she often seemed to regard with exasperation:

'Since last Sunday's dreadful news, we have seen, throughout Britain and around the world, an overwhelming expression of sadness at Diana's death.

We have all been trying in our different ways to cope. It is not easy to express a sense of loss, since the initial shock is often succeeded by a mixture of other feelings: disbelief, incomprehension, anger – and concern for those who remain. We have all felt those emotions in these last few days. So, what I say to you now, as your Queen and as a grandmother, I say from my heart.

First, I want to pay tribute to Diana myself. She was an exceptional and gifted human being. In good times and bad, she never lost her capacity to smile and laugh, nor to inspire others with her warmth and kindness. I admired and respected her – for her energy and commitment to others, and especially for her devotion to her two boys. This week at Balmoral, we have all been trying to help William and Harry come to terms with the devastating loss that they and the rest of us have suffered.

No one who knew Diana will ever forget her. Millions of others who never met her, but felt they knew her, will remember her. I for one believe there are lessons to be drawn from her life and from the extraordinary and moving reaction to her death. I share in your determination to cherish her memory.'

The broadcast thanked the mourners who had arrived with flowers, acknowledging that even if Diana was not a royal herself, the outpouring of grief had elevated her and given her a significance way beyond the divorced wife of Charles. In particular, the speech called for people to unite in grief and respect of Diana at her funeral:

'This is also an opportunity for me, on behalf of my family, and especially Prince Charles and William and Harry, to thank all of you who have brought flowers, sent messages and paid your respects in so many ways to a remarkable person. These acts of kindness have been a huge source of help and comfort.

Our thoughts are also with Diana's family and the families of those who died with her. I know that they too have drawn strength from what has happened since last weekend, as they seek to heal their sorrow and then to face the future without a loved one.

I hope that tomorrow we can all, wherever we are, join in expressing our grief at Diana's loss, and gratitude for her all-too-short life. It is a chance to show to the whole world the British nation united in grief and respect.

May those who died rest in peace and may we, each and every one of us, thank God for someone who made many, many people happy.'

Behind the Queen was an open window, and from it could be seen hordes of mourners who had gathered outside Buckingham Palace to pay their respects. It was a clever speech and some suspected that government advisers had helped hit the right note, acknowledging the public feeling while steering the people towards feeling unity and common cause with the Royal Family itself.

In spite of the Queen's well-crafted speech, Diana's death had opened up not just grief but questions.

The following day, the funeral of Diana took place and with it would come one of the most astonishing attacks on the modern Royal Family there had ever been.

CHAPTER 3

KEN WHARFE

'Are you my last line of defence?'

THERE IS ABSOLUTELY no doubt in my mind that Diana's abandonment of her British police security detail was the reason for her death. In my view, the security she had in Paris – or the lack of it – killed her. People can say, she must have known how to put a seatbelt on, and of course she did, but, like all Royals, she was used to being told to do things. Like all of them, she had got it into her system that someone would always tell her what the next step was. Previously, she would have expected us to be there, and would have been told to get in, go in that door and suchlike. In a way, we almost conditioned her. From my personal experience all members of the Royal Family rarely if ever interfered with the security advice. It's my belief that Diana's short time with Dodi Fayed was a very dark period for her, even without its tragic end, and that something as basic as putting a seatbelt on wouldn't even have occurred to her, as the life she had was changed beyond recognition from everything she had previously known.

I remember the first meeting I had with her at Kensington Palace. I arrived at Sandringham House in the mid-1980s to protect William and Harry, who were five and three years old respectively. At that point, I wasn't going to be assigned to Diana, I was there for the young princes. I was shown into a drawing room where Diana was sitting on the sofa. William was attempting to play a piano and Harry was being an entertaining pest, standing on a table, picking apart some lilies in a vase. Having been formally introduced by a butler, I did feel rather nervous, as would anyone. Immediately, Diana said to me, 'I don't envy you, Ken, looking after my kids – they can be a bloody nuisance.'

Her remarkably down-to-earth comment started a chain reaction. William turned round and declared, 'I'm not a ruddy nuisance!' Harry could barely speak properly but tried to join in before falling off the table as the vase broke. They ran off, as all children would do once they know they've done something wrong, pursued by Diana – and I hadn't even said anything yet!

Diana came back, a little out of breath. 'I'm so sorry, Ken – do you see what I mean?'

There wasn't this barrier between royalty and me, the policeman, the servant or whatever. It was more as though a sister or friend was speaking to me, and that was extraordinary. A short while later, I remember meeting her detective, the late Graham Smith, who agreed with me. 'That's exactly what she's like. It's not like working for the Queen, it's not like working for the Prince of Wales. She's different. She will emotionally involve herself and you have to be careful of that. You'll be stepping from the green to the red carpet. Diana will drag you in, not to embarrass you, but just as part of her style.'

I didn't really understand this at the time, but it became very clear exactly what he meant. Working with Diana's children, I saw how involved she was. She'd take them to school, always wanting to be there at the end of the school day. She would jig her appointments around her children; they were priorities for her. She didn't want them to be like other royal children, stuck in a nursery with a nanny. She wanted to be their mother.

For the next six months, my room was located very close to the nursery and I witnessed clearly Diana's relationship with her sons, as well as developing my own with the two young boys who would come to call me 'Uncle Ken'. Graham Smith, whose comments had alerted me to Diana's approach, sadly faced a battle with cancer which brought about my role as Diana's protection officer.

The very first public trip I had with her was to Majorca in Spain. She summoned me from my nearby hotel as I wasn't part of the protection detail at the Marivent Palace, and I dutifully arrived. The King of Spain had disappeared with the Prince of Wales and other guests, including the two young princes. Diana wanted to talk, and as she confided in me while we sat by a swimming pool, I wondered what my boss might say about the situation in which I now found myself.

'I wanted to tell you about my life, my situation and my marriage,' she began. 'I'm currently in a relationship with a man called James Hewitt.' *Why do I need to know this*? I wondered. Well, I knew it anyway, but did I need to know it from her. Actually, it was incredibly useful as it made me understand the Princess of Wales even more, having only known her a few months. She created a chemistry with almost everyone she met, and I wasn't immune. I knew quite a lot about her, yet she knew very little about me, although that changed as the months progressed. Indeed, because of her revelations to me in Spain, I felt I knew more about her than her husband did at that point. That brought me a lot closer to seeing how the mechanics of this woman worked.

When we returned to London, I felt closer to her because of what she had told me, and it would feel perfectly natural when she would ask me, on many occasions, about many things, 'What do you think of that, Ken?' Instead of accepting a 'cop-out' answer – 'It's nothing to do with me, sorry' – Diana expected an answer with reason every single time.

The role I had to play was markedly different to the ones expected of my colleagues placed in other royal protections. Having been a police officer for so many years, I now had to become a very different version of myself. Throughout my time in royal protection, senior management couldn't really understand my role, despite them being the ones who had put me there in the first place. They didn't understand the chemistry and the character of the woman I was working for, or the people we were all working for there. Royal protection is different now; it's changed dramatically but, in those days, it most certainly wasn't what I'd initially expected. I hadn't thought for one moment that I would be involved in such personal conversations – and there were times when I'd rather not have been involved at all; I'd have preferred to just get on with the protection side. Yet I realised, as time went on, that the openness of the Princess actually made the protection I could give even more secure because the trust and honesty was so complete, I was told everything by her. And I mean *everything*.

Information is power in any business, but particularly in my line of work – the more you know, the better. Throughout the time I had with Diana, never once was security dangerously compromised, because the information and intelligence I had from the woman herself was so great it allowed things to be near perfect.

I did find myself becoming almost a counsellor to Diana as she would frequently say, 'What do you think? What would you do? Am I doing this right?'

I think that for all of us, when we have an opinion based on our own experience, we can see something so obviously not right. So when asked any question, you can play it one of two ways: you can steadfastly refuse to answer, but if you feel the answer is going to be helpful, then in my opinion you have a duty to answer. That I happened to be advising a princess was irrelevant, given the relationship issues she fostered. I did find myself wondering, *Is this a new Ken?*

When I was a police inspector in London in the 1980s, it was a very difficult time. Margaret Thatcher was the Prime Minister and there was a lot going on. There were inner-city disturbances in Tottenham, Brixton, Bristol, Birmingham and Liverpool, there was the miners' dispute, and the country in general was in a pretty bad way. I was dealing with angry people everywhere, but I wasn't sorting out personal problems. In Tottenham, I was standing behind a shield arresting people under extraordinary circumstances, and then I was being abused by angry miners in Yorkshire. Eventually, later in the 1980s, I had become so disillusioned with policing that I moved onto royal protection, finding myself in a completely different world. But even though my new environment was removed from the 'real' world of policing, my earlier experiences of policing were to prove invaluable, if only in having the right contacts for intelligence and insight. My experience was of tremendous value, but I never for one moment thought I was back to where I'd been because I most certainly was not. The policing enabled me to solve certain problems away from Diana, through dialogue with local police services but, in a way, I did become a different man.

By the autumn of 1987, the relationship between Charles and Diana was at a tremendously low ebb. She once asked me, 'Ken, are you basically my last line of defence?' and I felt she was asking me a question of emotional support in the same way that she might expect me to take a bullet for her. I always tried to be as honest with her as possible, and that was something she desperately needed at that time. Despite everything that was going wrong in her marriage, she never took her eye off the ball when it came to her sons. From my early days, protecting the boys, I could already see that she was a very different sort of royal mother, which was particularly relevant to how I could help her.

William was five and attending pre-preparatory school in London while Harry was at nursery at Jane Mynors' School. Diana had meticulously planned this kind of education for her sons as she wanted her children to be raised in a completely different way from the nannying style Charles had been through behind closed doors of the Palace. Diana was never going to allow that. Whether the Prince wanted that or not, I can't be certain, but she most certainly wanted her children to lead 'as normal a life as possible'. The word 'normal' rang through all my time with her. *I want to be normal. Things have to be normal.* Of course, we know that within the framework of a royal palace, there is nothing normal, but it was all relative.

In Diana's eyes, going to a school like everyone else – albeit a privileged, fee-paying, pre-preparatory school in north London – was her idea of normal as it meant her sons could be with other boys of a similar status within society. She also wanted to take the children to school and to be seen to be taking them to school. Her ideal was to do the 'school run' whenever she could, and to her credit, she did exactly that whenever she could. She'd arrive at school very underdressed – often in jeans or a tracksuit if she wasn't going to an engagement – and by way of contrast, it was amusing to see the majority of other parents so smartly dressed in case they met the Princess!

The Prince of Wales would take William to school occasionally, but it was Diana who desperately wanted to do this. It wasn't in the psyche of Charles as much as her because I remember his attitude was, 'We have a nanny, we have a chauffeur – why wouldn't they do all of that?'

Unless there were engagements or foreign visits, Diana genuinely did do the school run, certainly for the first three or four years of their education. She enjoyed that and had a very good relationship with the headmistress as well as a jocularity with the teachers which they appreciated.

I remember one occasion when the music master, an Australian, was playing the piano at morning reception. Harry was sitting on the floor next to him and kept tugging his trousers.

'Stop it, Harry, stop it,' he urged him.

'Sir, sir!' he kept saying.

'Stop it! Stop pulling my trousers, Harry! What's the matter?'

'Sir, I can see your willy!' came the joke reply.

That completely put him off his playing and he told the

headmistress! She came to me and said, 'What shall we do about this, Ken?'

'Nothing! It's a five-year-old doing something a bit naughty – it's certainly not worth alerting the Palace, is it? I'll deal with it. If you start putting things on paper or calling parents in, it'll be a nightmare.'

Later that day, I told the story to the Princess who howled with laughter. She thought it was one of the most entertaining real-life things she'd ever come across. I knew what would happen – she would need to make something of it.

The following day, she took both boys to school and there was the music master in the hallway saying good morning to everyone.

'Good morning,' she said.

'Good morning, Your Royal Highness – how are you?'

'I'm fine, thank you. Now – I gather Harry saw your willy yesterday?' And with that, she chatted with him, laughing with other assembled staff who all revelled in the fun of the moment.

However, Diana's sense of normality didn't extend to getting her sons ready in the morning. She would sometimes have breakfast up in the nursery with the children and, during that time, the nanny was a lady called Barbara Barnes. She was rather a strict woman who seemed to me to favour William more than Harry, which I couldn't understand as Harry was little more than a baby. As a result of that, I think Diana found her quite difficult – she was scrupulously fair with her own boys and never showed favour. Barbara Barnes was a strong lady with strong ideas and could be quite harsh in welcoming new faces into the household, which I think was a normality for household staff. Your longevity of service meant a lot. If you had been there longer, you had more status than someone with exactly the same job who had been there for less time. If you'd been there longer, you were more important – it was as simple as that. Barbara didn't enjoy a good relationship with Diana and ultimately left. Olga Powell then came in, a much older lady, who was I think very influential. She was an old-style nanny – quite strict but very fair. She was a bit like Diana's mother, so they got on well.

Olga wasn't averse to the odd swipe when she saw fit. The nursery was literally opposite my room, and I could hear everything. Olga was once dealing with William's behaviour over breakfast one day, and I heard her say sternly, 'William, I love you, yes I do, but I'm beginning not to like you… I'm beginning not to like you a lot.'

I knocked on the door and I said, 'Everything all right in here, Olga?'

'Yes, but you'd better go away as I'm having a difficult morning.'

Sometimes I'd hear Diana go in. She might say, 'What's all this noise in here? If this happens anymore, you won't be seeing me up here again,' or, 'If this doesn't stop, we won't be going out later.' She was just like any other parent, throwing out empty threats.

There was a normality there, I suppose – if you ignore the fact that they had a huge nursery in a palace with a nanny and other staff. Diana was very influential in getting things ready for school, but they would be dressed and cleaned by the nanny and they'd find their own way to the front door or come via the staff kitchen. It was part of Diana's style not to exclude the children from anywhere in the Palace and she wanted every member of staff to be part of this wider family. The Prince found that difficult; for him, staff had their place and the Royals had theirs, but that didn't work for Diana. She wanted the children to speak with the butler, the chefs and others. As in the normal, everyday life of other people, the kitchen was the focal point of the house and Diana's style was to sit on top of the chest freezer in the morning, reading the newspaper and eating a slice of toast with the chef. She wouldn't sit in the dining room alone; she'd go for the hub of the 'home'.

Everybody within the household had quite an important part to play. That was a very good education for the kids – they learned to be respectful, but they could sometimes be naughty. If they were rude to me, I wouldn't go to the father or the mother and say, 'Look, your son's been an absolute nightmare,' I'd deal with it myself and they knew there were certain limits with 'Uncle Ken'. Diana would make it clear: 'If any of my kids are naughty, you deal with them, don't come to me.'

I believe that what we witness with William and Harry now – more so William as we see more of him – is that their mother laid the foundation for the fathers they have become. I think William would be the first to acknowledge that interaction with household staff as a young boy moulded him to accept some sort of normality himself. They were raised in a household that could be fun despite all these servants. It was a far cry from the below-stairs servants of the Victorian or Edwardian days and it was something which Diana has left as a tremendous legacy.

CHAPTER 4

ROS COWARD

'God granted you but half a life.'

Charles Spencer's address at Diana's funeral, Westminster
Abbey, 6 September 1997

'I stand before you today the representative of a family in
grief, in a country in mourning before a world in shock.

We are all united not only in our desire to pay our respects
to Diana but rather in our need to do so. For such was her
extraordinary appeal that the tens of millions of people taking
part in this service all over the world via television and radio
who never actually met her, feel that they too lost someone
close to them in the early hours of Sunday morning. It is a
more remarkable tribute to Diana than I can ever hope to
offer her today.

Diana was the very essence of compassion, of duty, of

style, of beauty. All over the world she was a symbol of selfless humanity. All over the world, a standard bearer for the rights of the truly downtrodden, a very British girl who transcended nationality. Someone with a natural nobility who was classless and who proved in the last year that she needed no royal title to continue to generate her particular brand of magic.

Today is our chance to say thank you for the way you brightened our lives, even though God granted you but half a life. We will all feel cheated always that you were taken from us so young and yet we must learn to be grateful that you came along at all. Only now that you are gone do we truly appreciate what we are now without and we want you to know that life without you is very, very difficult.

We have all despaired at our loss over the past week and only the strength of the message you gave us through your years of giving has afforded us the strength to move forward.

There is a temptation to rush to canonise your memory, there is no need to do so. You stand tall enough as a human being of unique qualities not to need to be seen as a saint. Indeed to sanctify your memory would be to miss out on the very core of your being, your wonderfully mischievous sense of humour with a laugh that bent you double.

Your joy for life transmitted wherever you took your smile and the sparkle in those unforgettable eyes. Your boundless energy which you could barely contain.

But your greatest gift was your intuition and it was a gift you used wisely. This is what underpinned all your other wonderful attributes and if we look to analyse what it was about you that had such a wide appeal we find it in your instinctive feel for what was really important in all our lives.

Without your God-given sensitivity we would be immersed in greater ignorance at the anguish of AIDS and HIV sufferers, the plight of the homeless, the isolation of lepers, the random destruction of landmines.

Diana explained to me once that it was her innermost feelings of suffering that made it possible for her to connect with her constituency of the rejected.

And here we come to another truth about her. For all the status, the glamour, the applause, Diana remained throughout a very insecure person at heart, almost childlike in her desire to do good for others so she could release herself from deep feelings of unworthiness of which her eating disorders were merely a symptom.

The world sensed this part of her character and cherished her for her vulnerability whilst admiring her for her honesty.

The last time I saw Diana was on July 1, her birthday in London, when typically she was not taking time to celebrate her special day with friends but was guest of honour at a special charity fundraising evening. She sparkled of course, but I would rather cherish the days I spent with her in March when she came to visit me and my children in our home in South Africa. I am proud of the fact apart from when she was on display meeting President Mandela we managed to contrive to stop the ever-present paparazzi from getting a single picture of her – that meant a lot to her.

These were days I will always treasure. It was as if we had

been transported back to our childhood when we spent such an enormous amount of time together – the two youngest in the family.

Fundamentally she had not changed at all from the big sister who mothered me as a baby, fought with me at school and endured those long train journeys between our parents' homes with me at weekends.

It is a tribute to her level-headedness and strength that despite the most bizarre-like life imaginable after her childhood, she remained intact, true to herself.

There is no doubt that she was looking for a new direction in her life at this time. She talked endlessly of getting away from England, mainly because of the treatment that she received at the hands of the newspapers. I don't think she ever understood why her genuinely good intentions were sneered at by the media, why there appeared to be a permanent quest on their behalf to bring her down. It is baffling.

My own and only explanation is that genuine goodness is threatening to those at the opposite end of the moral spectrum. It is a point to remember that of all the ironies about Diana, perhaps the greatest was this – a girl given the name of the ancient goddess of hunting was, in the end, the most hunted person of the modern age.

She would want us today to pledge ourselves to protecting her beloved boys, William and Harry, from a similar fate and I do this here, Diana, on your behalf. We will not allow them to suffer the anguish that used regularly to drive you to tearful despair.

And beyond that, on behalf of your mother and sisters, I pledge that we, your blood family, will do all we can to continue the imaginative way in which you were steering these two exceptional young men so that their souls are not simply immersed by duty and tradition but can sing openly as you planned.

We fully respect the heritage into which they have both been born and will always respect and encourage them in their royal role but we, like you, recognise the need for them to experience as many different aspects of life as possible to arm them spiritually and emotionally for the years ahead. I know you would have expected nothing less from us.

William and Harry, we all cared desperately for you today. We are all chewed up with the sadness at the loss of a woman who was not even our mother. How great your suffering is, we cannot even imagine.

I would like to end by thanking God for the small mercies he has shown us at this dreadful time. For taking Diana at her most beautiful and radiant and when she had joy in her private life. Above all we give thanks for the life of a woman I am so proud to be able to call my sister, the unique, the complex, the extraordinary and irreplaceable Diana, whose beauty, both internal and external, will never be extinguished from our minds.'

(Reproduced by kind permission of Charles, Earl Spencer; the text can be found online at https://www.bbc.co.uk/news/special/politics97/diana/spencerfull.html)

Diana's funeral itself brought an extraordinary challenge from her brother, Charles Spencer, when he gave what is quite rightly considered one of the greatest speeches of all time. It so perfectly encapsulated what the public was feeling about how Diana had been let down, what she'd hoped for and who she was as a person. It is a perfect speech, each part paying tribute to the person Diana was, as well as summing up the public emotions around her death. Again, as with the Queen's words after Diana's death, it's rather important to recall exactly what Charles Spencer said within those hallowed confines of Westminster Abbey. Like the Queen, he emphasised the way Diana's death had united people, but his version of their grief was more dramatic. The people needed to pay their respects together. They felt they knew her. But he also raised a flag of disunity, introducing himself as a 'representative' of Diana's family, her other family, by implication her 'real' family.

Charles Spencer tells how he wrote the speech overnight. It flowed onto the page. Remarkable then that he found the precise words to capture how the public felt about Diana:

'Diana was the very essence of compassion, of duty, of style, of beauty. All over the world she was a symbol of selfless humanity. All over the world, a standard bearer for the rights of the truly downtrodden, a very British girl who transcended nationality.'

Again there was an implicit challenge and reminder of Diana's cruel treatment when stripped of her HRH title: 'Someone with a natural nobility who was classless and who proved in the last year that she needed no royal title to continue to generate her particular brand of magic'.

As the speech progressed, it touched on how Diana would be

remembered and was prescient about how there would be a struggle over her memory – a struggle based on false opposition between saints and sinners. Charles, knowing her as a brother, knew neither a saint nor a sinner but a complex, caring and fun human:

'There is a temptation to rush to canonise your memory, there is no need to do so. You stand tall enough as a human being of unique qualities not to need to be seen as a saint. Indeed, to sanctify your memory would be to miss out on the very core of your being, your wonderfully mischievous sense of humour with a laugh that bent you double.

Your joy for life transmitted wherever you took your smile and the sparkle in those unforgettable eyes. Your boundless energy which you could barely contain.

But your greatest gift was your intuition, and it was a gift you used wisely. This is what underpinned all your other wonderful attributes and if we look to analyse what it was about you that had such a wide appeal, we find it in your instinctive feel for what was really important in all our lives.'

The speech continued by recognising her work with the socially marginalised and ostracised. 'Without your God-given sensitivity we would be immersed in greater ignorance at the anguish of AIDS and HIV sufferers, the plight of the homeless, the isolation of lepers, the random destruction of landmines.' Charles then went on to acknowledge the deep connection Diana felt towards some of the marginalised people she met:

'Diana explained to me once that it was her innermost feelings of suffering that made it possible for her to connect with her constituency of the rejected.

And here we come to another truth about her. For all the status, the glamour, the applause, Diana remained throughout a very insecure person at heart, almost childlike in her desire to do good for others so she could release herself from deep feelings of unworthiness, of which her eating disorders were merely a symptom.

The world sensed this part of her character and cherished her for her vulnerability while admiring her for her honesty.'

Spencer's speech is personal and open. He acknowledges Diana's problems including her eating disorder. He also acknowledges difficulties in her own life, from a child shuttled between her divorced parents and later her life in the Royal Family 'the most bizarre life imaginable': 'It is a tribute to her level-headedness and strength that despite the most bizarre-like life imaginable after her childhood, she remained intact, true to herself.'

Spencer went on to address the media hounding of Diana which many people believed was one of the causes of her death:

'I don't think she ever understood why her genuinely good intentions were sneered at by the media, why there appeared to be a permanent quest on their behalf to bring her down. It is baffling.

My own and only explanation is that genuine goodness is threatening to those at the opposite end of the moral spectrum. It is a point to remember that of all the ironies about Diana, perhaps the greatest was this – a girl given the name of the ancient goddess of hunting was, in the end, the most hunted person of the modern age.'

With twenty-five years of hindsight and especially after the hounding of Harry and Meghan, the most painful parts of the speech are where Charles Spencer, a member of a family arguably older and grander than the Royal Family, also threw down a challenge: the boys' blood family – the Spencers – would see to it that they were not destroyed by media intrusion and hostility and that the journey started by Diana to raise different royal children would be continued:

'She would want us today to pledge ourselves to protecting her beloved boys, William and Harry, from a similar fate and I do this here, Diana, on your behalf. We will not allow them to suffer the anguish that used regularly to drive you to tearful despair.

'And beyond that, on behalf of your mother and sisters, I pledge that we, your blood family, will do all we can to continue the imaginative way in which you were steering these two exceptional young men so that their souls are not simply immersed by duty and tradition but can sing openly as you planned.'

It has turned out that William and Harry have had far more to do with the Royal Family than the Spencers. But at the time it touched a defiant chord. As did the concluding paragraph, which still resonates today:

'I would like to end by thanking God for the small mercies He has shown us at this dreadful time. For taking Diana at her most beautiful and radiant and when she had joy in her private life. Above all we give thanks for the life of a woman I am so proud to be able to call my sister, the unique, the complex, the extraordinary and irreplaceable Diana, whose beauty, both internal and external, will never be extinguished from our minds.'

I was in Hyde Park during the funeral service, having stood among the estimated two million people lining the route as Diana's body passed by. In itself this was an extraordinary experience, standing on a beautiful autumnal day in a deep silence broken occasionally by an involuntary sob. But many people who were in the Abbey itself tell their own spine-tingling story of when Diana's little brother finished his speech. First, there was a silence, and then no one could quite understand what the strange sound was which rolled in currents, washing across the seated mourners. Some thought it was rain, but it was actually people clapping, which moved forward like a wave from Hyde Park to the back of the Abbey. It was a spontaneous expression of emotion, of grief, love and recognition of themselves in Spencer's words.

It was most certainly an acknowledgement of the points raised by Charles Spencer and of the challenge he laid down. When he pledged to protect William and Harry, he was basically saying – in front of Charles, the Queen, and the rest of the Royal Family, *I won't let them do to your boys what was done to you.*

Charles Spencer had thrown down the gauntlet and it wasn't fanciful to feel a flutter of republican fervour at that moment.

Suddenly a discussion of that subject seemed pertinent, immediate even. People weren't about to storm the Bastille – this was Britain after all – but there was definitely something in the air.

The entire funeral had been extraordinary, starting with Diana's body on a horse-drawn gun carriage making its lonely way to St James's Palace, where William and Harry, Prince Charles, Prince Philip and Lord Spencer stepped out to walk behind it. Charles Spencer has stated that he believed he should be the only one to follow his sister's coffin and that the inclusion of her sons was 'bizarre' and not something she would have wanted. What was certainly unusual was that behind these frontline mourners were representatives from many of the charities Diana had worked with, people she had touched and helped. This was quite remarkable. Ordinary people were being given virtually the same status as the Royal Family in a spectacle watched by over two billion people across the entire world. It allowed an immediate conversation to develop about what she had done as people told their stories and a dialogue opened about her incredible achievements.

But Spencer's words also confirmed a growing realisation about how unhappy and vulnerable Diana had been after the divorce. He made it clear that the paparazzi had been behaving like a pack of hounds and that this had caused Diana great unhappiness in her life. Now it was clear to everyone that Diana had been struggling to create her own identity, to try to become her own person independent from her faithless husband, but had been treated so badly. Once she had no royal security, she fell victim to the uncontrolled behaviour of the paparazzi and the vindictive coverage of her life in the tabloids. The public had realised the extent of her unhappiness after the televised interview with Martin Bashir, which had taken place at the end of 1995, but now it was felt that what was perceived as her cold treatment by the Royal Family and Charles's cruelty were implicated in her death. Had it not been for this treatment she might not have died. Inevitably therefore any discussion of Diana brought with it questions of who the Royal Family were and of whether they deserved their position.

The Queen, through sheer longevity, and hard work, seems to have won back the affection she lost – and she did lose it through Diana's death – but it seems to me that questions over Charles's suitability have never gone away. Those questions erupted forcefully again during the Paul Burrell trial in 2002 and resurfaced in 2021 with the threat of charges against the Prince's former valet Michael Fawcett, who Diana viewed as a thorn in her flesh and a lead figure in what she called the 'B Team', that is, Charles's people. Scandals such as this and the Prince Andrew saga have continued to rock the monarchy, and seem to give ongoing credence to Diana's feeling that there was something rotten in the state of Denmark. So much information has come out corroborating her claims that not only was she was treated badly by some of these people, but that some of their behaviour may have been far from respectable. It seems astonishing that we are twenty-five years down the line from her death and there is still material coming forward which echoes her warnings from more than a quarter of a century ago.

The phenomenally successful television series *The Crown* introduced a whole new younger generation of viewers to the Diana story. Many of them are quite shocked, not having known the full story of Charles's adultery and Diana's unhappiness. Through this and other television and cinematic portrayals, Diana has passed into popular mythology. Her enduring appeal is both a testament to her star power and also indicative that the memory of her will not dissipate any time soon; and this is mainly because her life and death raised deeper as yet unresolved questions about the British establishment.

Ultimately the power of Charles Spencer's speech was that it allowed the public to see Diana as the extraordinary and charismatic woman she was, and understand the resistance she had encountered with the media and the British establishment. When Diana died there was a kind of realisation of just what she had been – which had been partly lost sight of in the media coverage of her private life. When I wrote about her in 2004, I talked to many hundreds of people who had known her well or had worked with her in her many charities. The level of awe they had of her ability to relate to ordinary people and those in extreme situations was enormous. It is by no means meant to trivialise serious situations and conditions, but there is no doubt she also brought glamour to many charities who would otherwise have been ignored or ostracised. Here was this woman who could do anything, who was on the cover of magazines and newspapers, who was the type who could sell huge numbers of copies of those magazines and newspapers simply because of what dress she was wearing, but she was speaking to them, she was connecting with them, in some cases befriending them.

Charles Spencer was right to emphasise her caring nature and her charisma, something he had known since they were children. Diana was genuinely charismatic. Everyone who met her noticed it and it was fully recognised when she died, when it was realised just how important she had been to so many people. People felt very complex emotions realising who she was and that she was the most potent thing the Royal Family had ever had. Diana had been far more thrillingly interesting to photographers, journalists and the public than anyone else. She had this extraordinary combination of glamour, charm and vulnerability and when she reached out to people through Andrew Morton's book and Martin Bashir's interview, the public heard *her* and her suffering. All of these elements made her the most fascinating, attractive member of the Royal Family they'd ever known within the ranks. Yet they appeared to have rejected her. Whether anyone will ever reach those dizzy – and for the monarchy, often terrifying – heights again remains to be seen.

CHAPTER 5

KEN WHARFE

'I can do what I like – I can do whatever I like.'

DIANA DID LOATHE formality – she found the rituals and stiffness of the Royal Family difficult, but they found her difficult too. She always wanted the children involved but there had to be certain protocols adhered to, which the Queen and Charles were welded to. If Diana thought of breaking any new ground, it was frowned upon. As audiences have watched the cinematic and televisual representations of Diana – indeed of the whole monarchy – in recent years, there has been a blurring of what actually happened, and much has passed into public consciousness, which almost certainly never occurred. In the Oscar-nominated 2021 film *Spencer*, for example, we saw an almost entirely fabricated version of her story.

I was actually alerted to the making of *Spencer* by the actor who played Charles. I've known Jack Farthing since he was eleven years old and he rang me up one day to ask, 'Would you be interested in talking me through certain aspects before I tackle this role, Ken?' Of course, I very much wanted to help him, but was contractually held in another project. All the same, I was interested in Jack's new acting role, and when I asked him what the film was about, he said, 'Oh Ken, you're not going to like it!' When I watched it, I could see why he said that.

I had to concede that Kristen Stewart did look a bit like Diana and certainly had mastered some of her mannerisms – such as the run across the field which was a decent approximation of just how Diana ran in the mothers' race at school – and she captured her sense of dolefulness and lack of interest while at the dining table. For me, though, a lot of it was totally wrong and rather bizarre. The opening scene shows the character of Diana driving alone and completely lost on her way to Sandringham – although the one place that Diana could find with her eyes shut was Sandringham House. The scene where the character met the chef outside a garage somewhere was nonsense, as was the suggested lesbian affair with one of her dressers. How it got made, never mind nominated for awards, was beyond me. In my view, nothing in the film could give the viewer a closer insight into Diana.

It seemed to me that it had not been researched adequately. It was a pastiche, a fable with a few elements of truth – for example, the boys did get their gifts on Christmas Eve rather than Christmas Day (although I suspect that the likelihood of Diana buying them something from a service station borders on zero). There was indeed a weighing machine at Sandringham, but I honestly don't know if that was brought out at Christmas to weigh guests as a method of ensuring they had eaten enough festive fare. The film implied that this was the case – it was to assure the hosts that events had been so enjoyable, they'd put on weight – but I believe the machine was an old Edwardian piece rather than a Windsor 'thing'. Another misleading aspect was that Diana had outfits laid out and labelled for every single interaction – in real life, she had two dressers, very charming women, but as she was generally opposed to formality, she would not have taken this approach. The Prince, on the other hand, would have all of his clothes 'put out' – two pairs of socks, two ties, two shirts, two pairs of underpants, and so on – all laid out by his valet.

Diana had a real problem with that. 'Why the hell can't my husband sort his own bloody wardrobe out?' she'd mutter.

She herself would go down to the dressing room and say to Evelyn or Faye, her dressers, 'I need a pair of jeans,' or, 'I'll wear that jumper, just put it in the room,' and they'd place them on a chair for her. The only time any outfit was bagged up would be on a foreign tour because of the transfer of items from the Palace to the airport to the destination; those would be placed in bags with the Diana cipher on them. That was as far as it went. She kicked against having every moment of her life laid out for her, but her husband had been raised with that. He knew nothing else and felt it was perfectly 'normal'. Diana was a very casual dresser in her own life – she would wear jeans quite often whereas the Prince of Wales did not. I remember one of the nannies – the late Ruth Wallace – came down in jeans one morning for breakfast and he went completely ballistic. Ruth cried over the interaction quite desperately and Diana was appalled by how her husband had behaved. Ruth was looking after children after all, and jeans seemed perfectly appropriate for that task. Those kinds of out-of-date traditions were very hard for Diana to take.

In terms of clothes, Diana was very hands-on in her design and choices. She had many fashion designers who wanted her favour of course, but Catherine Walker was her favourite. Catherine had a studio in Kensington and we'd go there on a fairly regular basis. She would suggest designs and Diana would be closely involved. The Princess was very selective and certainly wasn't too bothered about the cost, particularly when it came to foreign tours as there was a generous budget there for her to best represent the UK abroad. The Prince always found those costings rather difficult to swallow – God knows why, as he's the last person who should complain about it. Diana was actually very conscious of costs in other aspects of life, and she was always wondering about how much things were. I remember going to her favourite restaurant, San Lorenzo, where she would often meet friends for lunch. I would sit at the bar with a bowl of pasta which cost about eleven or twelve pounds in those days, quite a hefty price in the 1980s. One day, her friend was late in turning up and Diana beckoned me to sit with her. (As an aside, Diana was incredibly punctual – I never knew her to be late for anything, a real stickler for time.) I went over and, when her friend arrived, asked the second woman what she was having just to make conversation.

'I love the veal here,' she told me.

'That's a bit pricey,' I replied.

'What are you having?' she asked.

'Just the pasta.'

I went back to my lunch. When Diana had finished, she decided that she wanted to go shopping.

'I need to get some dresses for the Pakistan trip,' she told me.

We walked along Beauchamp Place, where Dale Tryon – one

of Charles's old flames – had a dress shop called 'Kanga', her own nickname. As we chatted, Diana asked me just as her friend had done, 'So, what did you have for lunch, Ken?'

'I had some pasta, Ma'am.'

'How much was that?'

'About eleven or twelve pounds.'

She pondered that for a moment then asked, 'Who pays for all of this?'

Wondering quite where this was going, I replied, 'Why are you asking me that?'

'I'm just interested.'

Without being flippant I said, 'Well – the taxpayer, Ma'am.'

This wasn't the first time she'd approached the subject and asked about costs, but I just laughed it off. We got into Kanga Tryon's shop and Diana tried on two silk dresses for a visit to Pakistan.

'What do you think?' she enquired.

'Stunning, absolutely stunning,' I told her, quite honestly.

'I thought I'd get the two of them, the pink and the green.'

'They'd be perfect for Pakistan,' I agreed. 'Fantastic. How much are they, just out of interest?'

'Don't tell anybody, Ken but they're three and a half thousand pounds each.'

'Who's paying for this?' I asked.

'Well, it's for Pakistan, Ken.'

'You mean the taxpayer? I tell you what, Ma'am, that's an awful lot of fucking pasta!'

To her credit, she did laugh. I'll never forget that day and have photographs of those very dresses. It's interesting to compare Diana's approach with how the media views Kate, the Duchess of

Cambridge, and what she wears. There is always an underlying tone that Kate is wary of how much she's spending and there is much talk of her 'recycling' outfits (which usually means she's worn them more than once), but I don't recall Diana's clothing being broken down financially the way hers is. It was a different time in the media – people expected Diana to look good and it was just expected these things would cost. I dare say she could have dressed in Primark's finest and would have come out looking wonderful anyway, but I do think there is something different about accountability and transparency nowadays. There really was none of that in the 1980s and 1990s.

The glamorous world of foreign trips and couture fashion was a far cry from the kind of normality Diana was keen to instil in William and Harry. During my time with her, we went to the cinema, to a burger bar, and had a ride in a London black taxi.

One day she said to me, 'Ken, I want to take them on the underground or on a bus.'

'Anything is possible, Ma'am,' I told her.

Within a few days I had arranged with her chauffeur the use of 'a daily runabout' vehicle.

'Drop us off at Hyde Park Corner, will you?' I asked Simon, the driver.

We arrived there and Harry got the underground tickets, very pleased with himself. We only went two stops along to Piccadilly Circus but there were certainly plenty of people looking at us – you never knew whether they had worked out who Diana was, or if they thought they were seeing a particularly good lookalike! On this occasion, though, with the boys in tow as well, it must have been pretty obvious.

Piccadilly had a bus lane that was going against the flow of traffic, a rather weird idea that worked for a while. We got on a Number 38 bus and there was a conductor, a Sikh man with a yellow turban. This was a source of much amusement to William and Harry, particularly Harry, as they had never seen such a figure as this fellow in their rarefied world. They couldn't quite work it out. We climbed up to the top deck and, within minutes, we had arrived at Green Park, where we got off. The conductor had recognised Diana and the children and was reluctant to take any money from them.

'No, no,' said Diana, 'you must let us pay for our tickets.'

Harry had a handful of coins which he handed over. As we got off, the conductor was standing on the platform and he said, 'Thank you very much for coming on my bus,' in a rather strong Indian accent.

Harry imitated him in his reply, saying, 'Thank you very much, putt dutt ding ding!'

Diana was highly embarrassed by that. When we all stepped onto the pavement, she lightly smacked him around the back of the head saying, 'Don't you ever do that again, Harry! That was extremely rude.'

Harry shrugged it off and we all went back to Kensington Palace. The following day, there was a short note from him on my desk that told me he liked me but that I could not sing, and ended with 'putt putt ding ding' followed by his name.

I think the incident shows that, at times, Diana had her struggles with parenting just like many other people. These days, she could never have gone on the bus or to the supermarket – she would have been photographed constantly on people's phones – in whatever age, she would have had naughty children to deal with – and I guess that is something that wouldn't have changed.

Her boys were not the only ones to cause her irritation at times. Mohamed Al-Fayed consistently pursued Diana for a variety of reasons. On a number of occasions, he offered her his house in the South of France and, towards the end of my time with Diana, she told me she was going there.

'It'll be great,' she told me, as if there was nothing to it at all. 'You can go and do a recce first, Ken.'

'I don't think it's a good idea.'

'What do you mean?'

'Have you discussed it with the Prince?'

'I can do what I like – I can do whatever I like. I don't need to talk about it with him.'

'I think you do. Have you discussed it with your private secretary?'

'No. This is a holiday, Ken.'

'I know that, but let's just talk this through.' I gave her my view: 'You know who Al-Fayed is, you know what he wants. I dare say he does like you, Ma'am, but he wants something back in return, these people generally do. It would suit him to say that his security was able to look after you and your two children. Here is a man who is desperate for British citizenship – you're going to put the government in a very compromising position. My answer is, first and foremost, speak to your husband about it. He'll go absolutely loopy, as you know he will – that's why you don't want to speak to him about it. But I'm telling you, if you do go ahead with this, without consulting anyone first, you will make it very difficult for yourself and the Royal Family. So my answer is, I won't go and I won't recommend it.'

Diana went off in a big sulk. I don't know who else she spoke to, but a week later she came back to me, and said – beginning with her usual words, 'As you know, I can do what I like – but you're probably right. I won't go.'

I could connect with Diana on matters like that. There were times when she simply didn't want to go on engagements. 'I can't go to Bristol, I can't go to Newcastle,' she would declare.

'Don't go then – but why don't you want to go?' I would say. 'Think about it. It's nothing to do with me. As you keep telling me, you can do what you like. But you're going to disappoint three, four, five thousand people who have been waiting for this as it's been planned in the Lord Lieutenant's diary for months. These are the people you'll let down. You are an actress. This is a piece of theatre for you and all you need to do is perform. You're brilliant at it, which is why you're so popular. Even though you don't feel like doing it, you have to do it unless you are seriously ill.'

And she would go. She really was a consummate performer. Diana knew that there were certain things expected of her and she would often have to act, but there was a completely natural and genuine side to her which shone through in her interactions with ordinary people. This is what made her who she was, and this is why we still remember her to this day.

CHAPTER 6

ROS COWARD

*'I think it's the strength that causes the
confusion and fear.'*

WHEN DIANA DIED one of the themes which emerged
from the mourners and commentators was about how
she had modernised the monarchy, how she had made it inevitable
that the Royal Family should change. Her style was relaxed and
informal and her contact with people direct and unstuffy. She'd
taken on risky charities that the Royal Family had previously
avoided: AIDS, Leprosy, and Landmine campaigning to name but
a few. She had thrown herself into a different kind of mothering
too, determined to raise her boys differently from the usual formal
royal upbringing.

With Meghan's marriage to Harry in 2018 it was tempting to
conclude that Diana's approach had prevailed, and that, even if
not recognised in her own lifetime, her approach had changed the
British Royal Family beyond all recognition.

Meghan and Harry's wedding in Windsor was, after all, an

extraordinary affair, with many modern elements. Remarkably, in the absence of Meghan's father, Prince Charles walked her down the aisle. He also accompanied to her seat, Meghan's mother, an Afro-American woman who, in the absence of Meghan's father, had to assume a more prominent role. Some of this came about because of the breakdown in Meghan's family relations. There was the alienation of the bride's father, which created so much ill will, and something which clearly should have been mediated by the Palace, who ought to have maintained an effective channel of communication. But whatever the cause, and bewildering though it seemed to be to some members of the Royal Family, the outcome was an occasion which seemed to embrace the modern multicultural world and offered a vision of a new kind of monarchy even more radical than that envisaged by Diana. The service paid tribute to Meghan's black heritage, with a gospel choir, a black preacher, and a talented young black cellist.

Yet, only three years later Harry and Meghan had left Britain and were telling the world via an interview with Oprah Winfrey that they had been compelled to escape Britain because of the media harassment of Meghan and the Royal Family's indifference to Meghan's fate. Echoing Diana's views, Harry wistfully regretted how he and Meghan had felt trapped. In fact, he added that the other members of his family were also trapped in their attitudes, they just didn't know it.

Meghan and Diana share certain qualities. Both women cut through the pomp and circumstance, managing to touch so many excluded groups. Meghan was gold dust for a multicultural Britain negotiating its role in the world post-colonially and they let her slip from their hands – maybe the lessons of Diana haven't been learned at all. Meghan, until the British press turned on her, was attracting the same kind of interest as Diana. Glamorous, controversial and interesting, she had the potential to challenge the Royal Family in their ways and assumptions and have a compelling public presence.

Both women attracted jealousy from other members of the Royal Family. Diana became the focus of people's interest in royalty and upstaged them in many ways. But instead of recognising that, they didn't harness or support it. Instead, she was left struggling with intense public scrutiny without royal support. There was no attempt to harness her popularity. The Royal Family didn't use it at all, and there has been a similar pattern with Meghan. One thing Diana didn't have to deal with personally – although she did later on in terms of her relationships – was the issue of race, which has clearly been a huge bone of contention in Meghan's and Harry's minds with her lack of integration into the Royal Family. It was during the Oprah Winfrey television interview in 2021 that we first heard the allegation that Meghan and Harry had been asked what colour their as yet unborn baby, Archie, would be, and they seemed to imply this wasn't the first time something had been mishandled (not that it should be suggested that racism is a 'mishandling').

Both women were strong and independent, although in very different ways, and this may have been at the root of the jealousy they experienced. Meghan's strength comes from her career as a successful actress. Diana's journey to independence and strength came from a struggle to free herself from many of the expectations of her background: her journey towards becoming a different type of mother and woman was key.

It's tempting to wonder if the birth of Harry in 1984 was the moment when the reality of Diana's situation dawned on her fully. There had been a sort of period of grace with Diana's second pregnancy when she was carrying Harry. For about four months she and Charles were relatively calm with each other which, ironically, followed a period when she had started to get very suspicious of his return to Camilla. Diana said that her second pregnancy was a miracle as she and Charles spent very little time together, and the pair certainly seemed to return to their somewhat toxic status once the baby was born. Charles is alleged to have said, 'It's another boy.'

Diana had known the sex of their child all along, but she also knew that Charles wanted a girl, and so had kept quiet. That was one of the death knells for the relationship. The period in between the births of the two boys was, as she said, full of darkness despite a calmness with Charles. Emotionally and mentally, things were hard. Yet it was to propel her forward on a journey of self-discovery and what makes the journey all the more remarkable was that she was ill-equipped to undertake it.

There were very few people Diana could turn to. The Duchess of York, Sarah Ferguson, put herself forward as a natural shoulder to cry on, but the relationship between the pair was a turbulent one. There had always been a lot of press gossip about Diana getting up to jolly japes with Sarah Ferguson, especially once her days were on a separate path from Charles, who was clearly going about his old life. Diana had undoubtedly imagined that, once they were married and had children, they would be a family of sorts, but Charles was on a different pathway – the one which existed before the marriage and which would continue. Fergie was a strange person who has somehow escaped some of the scrutiny around Prince Andrew but she too seems to have had inappropriate links to odd people who on certain occasions appear to have given or loaned her money.

Her book – *My Story* – suggests a superficial woman who dragged Diana into a 'we're girls together against the stuffy Royals' notion, which has some truth to it, but also didn't do Diana any favours or help her find a way of living with Charles. Diana was much more dutiful and had wanted to find a solution that would allow her to continue with her royal duties.

Diana was incredibly young when she married and had her sons. The public were delighted when she fell pregnant as that meant the soap opera would continue, but they were aware of her age – she was only twenty-one when William was born, which was almost a gymslip mother in that day and age, even forty years ago. She was barely out of her teenage years when she'd had a crush on Charles, and the fantasy of living happily ever after with children was clearly front and centre of that romantic vision. When she was then pregnant with Harry quite soon after, there was an ever-increasing public interest in her, which must have been quite overwhelming for her, as all women do feel somewhat vulnerable at that point in their lives. Having children was obviously very much what she wanted – she was naturally someone who had always thought that motherhood would be central to her life, but experiencing it through a constant prism of press and public interest, at a time when the reality of her relationship with Charles was dawning on her, was a huge pressure.

Diana's route to redefining her life was always going to be difficult. She lacked education. She was bright but not at all academic. Apparently, she regretted having said to a child, to reassure him, that she was as 'thick as two short planks'. Camilla also only got one O-level but never drew attention to this. But it's certainly true that Diana lacked the kind of education which might have led to a career, and she clearly expected her primary role to be as wife and mother. She was very maternal and had been extremely protective of her younger brother (whom she fussed over like a mother hen) and motherhood was pretty much her destiny. While she was at West Heath School, Diana's music teacher Penny Walker had a baby. She told me that Diana appeared on her doorstep with a present almost as soon as the child was born, and was incredibly attentive and interested in the baby. Significantly she was also the first babysitter, the only girl in the school the teacher would have trusted.

Everyone says, without exception, just how important the boys were to Diana and how they were her priority. She did try to give them as normal an upbringing as was possible within their class and their circumstances and obviously took on board what Charles had said about his own misery at Gordonstoun, deciding quite absolutely that would not be the path for her sons. William was the first royal to go to an ordinary school in London – not ordinary for most of us, but for Royals, it was exactly that.

While royal observers are pretty much of a mind with regards to Charles's upbringing, there is less unanimity when it comes to Diana's. Was it her more ordinary upbringing that sowed the seeds for her journey from a young woman bound by conventions to a strong, independent woman determined to raise her sons more normally? In 2004, I interviewed Diana's mother, Frances Shand Kydd, who like her daughter was very attractive, naturally elegant and politely welcoming, despite being in the grip of a debilitating illness. But from her comments to me, it was clear she felt defensive, and believed both she and her daughter had been misrepresented. Shand Kydd asserted – and her son Charles Spencer corroborated this – that when she divorced and moved to the island of Seil on the west coast of Scotland, the children did have ordinary lives there with her in the holidays. She says they came with friends to a normal house, not a stately home or palace or a grace-and-favour home on a royal estate, just somewhere they could be outside, playing as much as they wanted.

Like her own childhood, Diana's approach to motherhood was a cocktail of elements from what she had experienced as a child as well as Charles's world. She did have a lot of advantages, financially, a level of privilege, a lifestyle of ponies and swimming pools, but if you look at the chronology of her childhood, it was pretty fractured from an early age. The divorce happened when she was eight years old and her mother fought for custody, which she lost. There are some suggestions that Frances Shand Kydd may have hidden a lot from the children, and her relationship with Johnny, Earl Spencer, was certainly very problematic. It wasn't just that they had a cold divorce, there were all sorts of suggestions that there may have been other issues – certainly a well-known novel by domestic-violence campaigner Erin Pizzey was said to be based on Frances Shand Kydd. Diana never talked about this side of things, of seeing anything of that kind, and it does seem like both parents were pretty committed to the children. However much privilege there was and however much the parents attempted to shield the children, it was a difficult childhood however – emotionally, it was a difficult path to chart and a lot of Diana's insecurities appear to have come from that. Diana often spoke of wanting to protect her own children from divorce and never wanted to divorce Charles.

In terms of her own mothering, she was determined to give William and Harry the stability and security she didn't have – although, ironically, what followed was a repetition of it. As regards the so-called normality, which is often discussed, this is partly a reaction to the fact that Diana didn't have an especially privileged upbringing, or not a rarefied one like that of children of the Royal Family. For example, Diana would never have countenanced the nanny bringing out the baby to see its parents for a short period of the day, a practice espoused by the Royal Family. It sounds as if Charles had the kind of upbringing where he was brought down and presented to his parents, but largely stayed in the nursery at all other times when at home. In spite of some pictures of them having fun, it was a pretty chilly upbringing and Charles himself has spoken of that. Diana just didn't want to have that for her children, she wanted a hands-on experience, she didn't expect to immediately hand her baby over to someone else, she wanted to be a modern mother.

Within a lifestyle that belongs to the upper classes and, in her case, was overlaid by royalty, with all its duties and complications, there was always going to be conflict for Diana, who was naturally informal. There is an account from one of the mothers from Wetherby Prep School that she really did bring the children to school every day when she could, she did the school run, she joined in all the occasions and events. It doesn't sound very much to us, but in her class and milieu that was certainly making a statement. She didn't wash her hands of her kids, she wanted them around, playing near her, and there are lots of lovely accounts of the boisterous ways they had. It can't be denied that motherhood was Diana's forte and that she finally managed to break some of the ingrained rules and traditions around the Royals' approach to children and their upbringing.

One of the first photos of Diana after her engagement was taken at the nursery where she worked. On that day, she told the press that they could have one picture but she wanted some children around her for reassurance. The nursery manager had to hastily ask the parents for permission, which was granted, and then there was the famous account of the photographers moving Diana into a new position. In it, the sun was coming from behind, her dress looked slightly transparent and you could see her legs. It's one of the key iconic images of this young woman standing in the sunlight with children and looking very lovely, hinting at sexuality and future fertility. The frenzied interest which then followed Diana for the rest of her life was an indication that the Royal Family are scrutinised for their maternal roles and behaviour.

Once Diana had her boys, she said she'd done her duty, she'd produced an 'heir and a spare'. It was a joke but also an acknowledgement of the pressure she was under to conform, and the difficulty she would meet from within the Royal Family for her attempts to craft her own life differently, including the way she mothered her children. The contrast with Kate is striking.

Kate has very much done it all properly, she has provided two boys and a girl, but they have played it quite differently from Diana. Unlike Diana, she has been able to shield her children more. The Queen's Platinum Jubilee was the first time the public had been allowed such a prolonged public appearance of the children. There were far more pictures available of William and Harry, and far more recordings of events and relaxed occasions than there are of their children. Sometimes there was a suggestion that Diana tipped off the press when she took the boys out and maybe she did, but so what? It was usually negotiated with the photographers in quite a casual way – if you aren't intrusive, we'll get you some nice pictures at, for instance, Thorpe Park. Kate has stayed much more in control of the images of George, Charlotte and Louis. She is the one who takes the photos, she doesn't have open sessions – there aren't actually that many informal photographs of them as there were with William and Harry. We have very little knowledge of those children and there are even fewer of Archie and Lili. Diana allowed far greater public access to her children with the result that the public felt familiarity with Diana and her children and had a sense of their personalities.

Looking back, what is evident is that initially Diana had a degree of trust in the media around her children, which was often misplaced. One photographer has written that he witnessed the paparazzi harassing not only her but also harassing the kids. In 1995 she told Bashir, 'I've never encouraged the media. There was a relationship which worked before but now I can't tolerate it because of the harassment.' She became much more protective, but at first there was that degree of trust in the way she exposed them and her mothering to the royal press which you don't see in the same way around William and Kate, or Harry and Meghan. Kate is perceived as always doing everything right – and even more so since Meghan came along. Kate is increasingly presented by the media as the perfect royal wife, she causes no bother, she isn't struggling with an eating disorder. She isn't Diana. Meghan on the other hand has often been portrayed as 'trouble' – she rocks the boat, she has raised the issue of possible racism within the Royal Family, she has been there as Harry has tried to make a different life for himself. However, humans being humans, a lot of people actually prefer the complicated, the multi-faceted women that Diana was and Meghan is. They are sympathetic to the women who have, sometimes through necessity, attempted to remake their own lives and find meaning, journeys which apparently unsettle the Royal Family. As Diana rather presciently said, 'I think it's the strength that causes the confusion and fear.'

CHAPTER 7

KEN WHARFE

'He doesn't love me, he loves that woman.'

TOWARDS THE END of the 1980s and the start of the 1990s, Diana felt she'd had enough. She felt that she was propping up the popularity of the Prince of Wales and she was right. There's no doubt about it – she was far more popular than her husband. I remember that every day was massive in terms of news coverage and, if you were to scan over it now, you would see just how extraordinary the reaction was. Nowadays you might get the odd tea party if a member of the Royal Family visited, whereas entire streets were closed for Diana. That simply doesn't happen these days.

I remember coming back from an engagement early one afternoon and driving through the gates of Kensington Palace. As we arrived, the Prince of Wales was about to leave to go on an engagement, just him and his bodyguard.

'Have you had a nice day?' he muttered as they passed each other.

'Fantastic,' Diana replied. 'Where are you off to?'

'Oh, I have to go to my churches in the city.'

'You'll like that though! Do you want me to come with you?'

'No, I don't!' he erupted. 'They'll only be interested in you.'

That was the crux of it.

'Okay, I was only trying to help,' Diana said. We went inside and she commented to me, 'You see what I mean?'

'Yes … I can understand what he's saying though.'

She shot a look at me – perhaps that comment made me seem to be protecting the other side and this was the problem. There was almost a Tudor feel to life with them. There was an element of 'them and us', Charles's court and Diana's court within one *single* court. She referred to it as the 'A Team' and the 'B Team'; naturally, hers was the 'A Team'. So much of that was, of course, predicated around the Camilla 'issue'. The Prince's relationship with Mrs Parker Bowles was an open secret, although no one really supported Diana's obvious awareness of it. Although Diana had been very trusting of me from the start with the way she told me of her own affair with James Hewitt, Charles and Camilla were more of an understanding than anything else – whatever it was they had together was simply accepted. When Diana commented or reacted against it, she was the one who was made to feel she was in the wrong.

On a trip to Lech, in Austria, in 1992, I saw elements of their maritally estranged relationship play out yet again. Diana would go skiing in Austria every year and the Prince would ski in Klosters in Switzerland, and ne'er should the two ever meet. They had their separate courts there too.

One Friday evening, I received a phone call from my colleague, Tony Parker, who worked for the Prince of Wales.

'Wharfie, I've got an unusual request for you.'

'Go on …'

'Can you ask the boss lady if it's okay if the Prince comes and skis with his sons?'

'This is a first – I'll ask her but I don't see this working, to be honest with you. When does he want to come?'

'Tonight.'

All I could think was, *There's nowhere for him to stay.* I went to see Diana and said, 'Ma'am, you're probably not going to believe this, but the Prince has just asked, through Tony Parker, if he can come and spend two days skiing with William and Harry.' I left her out of it as she would have realised there was no way he would have wanted to go skiing with her anyway.

'Ken, I don't have a problem with that,' she told me. 'I can't stop him seeing his children – but he's not staying with me.'

'I'll sort that out as long as you're happy with it.' I was surprised – I thought this was her hallowed turf. I spoke to the hotelier, an extraordinary man called Hannes Schneider, who was known as Mr No Problem. 'Where can we put the Prince of Wales?' I asked him. Without even thinking, he decided to kick his cheese sommelier out of his room on the ground floor in order to vacate it for Charles. The Prince eventually arrived with his private secretary, his press secretary and a valet – the complete opposite to Diana, who travelled without that sort of entourage. Anyone official was out of bounds on her private holidays, which was why everything was left to me to sort out. Charles was shown his room while the others were billeted outside the hotel. Just before the others left, the Prince suddenly turned to Schneider and said, 'There's no fridge here!'

Well, this was effectively a servant's room, with little chance of there being a fridge! Schneider couldn't work out why he would want a fridge – this was a six-star hotel, all he would have had to do was ring a bell and everything would have been dropped to his door within a matter of seconds.

'Why do you want a fridge, Your Royal Highness?' he asked in his wonderful Austrian accent.

'Richard …' he replied, pointing to his private secretary, who produced a small bottle of clear liquid.

'For the bottle?' asked Schneider.

'Yes. It's my own martini mix.'

This was just the sort of thing that used to drive Diana mad. Schneider disappeared and then reappeared almost immediately carrying a small fridge on his shoulder, which we put in next to the single bed. Everyone moved on and the following day, Charles skied with the boys and even had lunch with Diana. At times like that, you would wonder, hang on, could this be the start of a reconciliation? One would never know.

But then a tragedy happened. Diana's father, John Spencer, died on the second day of Charles's visit to Lech and they had to cut short their holiday and return home. It fell to me to tell Diana of her father's death because it was felt that I was the person closest to her on the trip. She was calm when I first broke the news, but the tears soon began to flow. She began to sob, asking me, over and over again, 'What am I going to do, Ken, what am I going to do?' My heart went out to her – in that moment, Diana was nothing more or less than a young woman who had to face the loss of her father. I put my arms around her, desperate to comfort her, seeing a lost little girl rather than a princess.

I knew that, not only did I need to be there for her, but I also had to broach the matter of what came next and raise the issue of her husband.

'You can tell the Prince that I'm not travelling back with him,' Diana asserted. 'I want to go back but I want to go alone. He doesn't love me, he loves that woman – why should I help save his face now? It's too late for him to start acting like he cares. He's not coming.'

I said, 'We've been down this road before, I don't really think you have any choice.'

'Oh yes, I do. I can do what I want, Ken.' I'd heard that many times before and I would continue to hear it many more.

'I don't dispute that, but is this right?'

Charles's private secretary wouldn't speak to her about it. He was not flavour of the month with Diana either. I had a conversation with him in the private hallway of the hotel to work out how we would convince them to return to London together. There must have been 60 or 70 of the world's press outside who all knew about Earl Spencer's death and would be recording everything.

I got on perfectly well with Charles. Despite the difficulties with the marriage, he was incredibly generous to me and the staff; it was not my place to make any moral judgement on what he was doing with Camilla. He knew that I could talk to Diana in a way he could not, even saying to me at one point in his grimacing way, 'You know her better than me. Can you persuade her? We can't go back separately for this. I'm representing the Queen after all.'

'I understand that completely, Sir,' I told him – and I did. I went back to Diana's room with my colleague Dave Sharp, where we spoke to Diana for about two hours.

I suddenly had a brainwave. 'Ma'am, you know, your father

was the Queen's equerry and knew her well before your marriage. Just imagine how he would advise the Queen in a similar situation, because that's what it comes down to. For all the hurt I know this will bring you, it's ultimately about the Queen. You've always said you work for her; she has your loyalty. She would expect you and your husband to travel back to London together. You have to go back with the Prince; you just have to go with it.'

That is what sold it. Weeping, Diana agreed to travel back with Charles beside her and we left the following day. I sat in the front of the car as Tony Parker drove us back to Zürich to pick up the Queen's flight. As we passed through Zürs, the beauty of the deep snow and bright sun was in stark contrast to the grief of Diana, who was in floods of tears. The Prince looked out of the window and merely commented, in what seemed to be an offhand way, 'Look at this wonderful snow – what a terrible shame we've got to go back.'

Other than that rather unthinking comment – said as if Diana was merely having to cut short a rather fun holiday for an unimportant reason – there was silence in the car. Still, it worked, as the next day saw newspaper headlines stating that Charles had been by her side in her hour of need. The truth was, as soon as they returned to Kensington Palace, Charles went to Highgrove and Diana to pay her last respects to her father. By the time of Earl Spencer's funeral, two days later, things between the royal couple were in a bad way yet again. It seemed to me that Diana might erupt at any moment, and no one would be able to control her. Again, she hadn't wanted Charles to make the trip to Althorp for the funeral and when he arrived by helicopter, I could see that her fury and grief were combining in a potentially explosive cocktail.

'He's going to turn my father's funeral into a charade, Ken,' she said to me at one point.

'Ma'am, – just don't let him,' I replied, hoping that she would see her own behaviour would be much more likely to colour the day if she did indeed let loose on her husband.

As it transpired, Charles only stayed for the funeral, leaving Diana alone both before and after the ceremony. Her siblings were, of course, there – but her body language screamed that she was a woman alone. When we finally left Althorp, with Diana's father entombed in the vault of the Spencer ancestors, none of us could have known that just five years later, it would be the Princess of Wales herself who would be making that final journey too.

Of course, Diana's concerns about 'that woman' had been present for some time – in fact, it's hard to think of a point when they did not exist. She was always fearful whenever we went to Highgrove at the weekend and had to return with the children, because she knew (from staff) that, soon after she left, Camilla would arrive. She was actually on the money with Camilla, and there were eventually many people telling her what was happening as well as her own observations as, due to the approachable way she was with the staff, they were very keen to release snippets of information to her. Added to that, Highgrove and Kensington in comparison to Buckingham Palace are much smaller set-ups where there weren't endless miles of corridors – Highgrove was effectively a small country house where everybody knew everybody else's business, which aided gossip.

One day, Diana – instead of leaving Highgrove and turning right – turned left and drove up into Tetbury. Surprised by this left turn, and assuming she was planning an alternative route back to

Kensington Palace, I said to her, by way of a joke, 'Do you know a quicker way home?'

My warning signal levels were raised and I thought, *Hang on, there's an agenda here if we've changed plan.* For a moment, I couldn't work it out. My crew behind me must have wondered where the hell we were going. 'Drop back and just give me plenty of space,' I told them on the radio. Tetbury wasn't far away and after one circumnavigation of this small Cotswold town, Diana said, 'I want to go back to the house.'

'Really? Do you really want to do that?' I said. 'I now know why you want to return. Do it if you must but I suggest you don't engage in any conversation when you're there as it'll upset you. If you do go back and see Camilla's car there then you can satisfy yourself that you were right in thinking that when you leave, she turns up. But I suggest you leave it there, so as to avoid a confrontation.'

We did go back. When we passed through the police-manned security post the police officer, who was visually unsure as to what to do next, saluted Diana's passing and through my internal rear-view mirror I could see him scramble for the telephone. This was a normal practice informing the butler of her imminent arrival. Camilla's car was parked immediately outside the front door.

We paused for a moment with Diana locked in silence, this was very painful for her. I said: 'Ma'am, I know how you feel – you have rightly confirmed what you have always thought. Let's go back to London.'

We drove straight back out again. It was a dance which had begun before Diana's time and it would be one which played out for many years to come.

She knew all along that these liaisons were taking place – I mean, the fact that they were even taking place at Highgrove showed how open the secret was. Fairly high people within the establishment knew, mainly Royals and friends of the Prince of Wales, who had knowledge of his relationship with Camilla before he even married Diana. There weren't many people on his side who were understanding or wanted to be understanding of the plight of the young Princess of Wales and what she was experiencing – they were loyal to the Prince. It was the same with Andrew Parker Bowles – he was very much aware of the fact that his own wife was having an affair with the Prince of Wales and was perfectly happy with that. That was the establishment way. He was an army brigadier whose attitude was pretty much, 'Oh, so my wife's having an affair with the Prince of Wales? That's all right – I'll go and do something else.' It was that sort of world, that sort of attitude in that section of society.

It was an eye-opener to me – you see so much and people behave so differently. What was no different at all, however, was that at the centre of everything was a wife and mother who felt utterly alone, betrayed by her husband and without a shred of support from the Royal Family. I watched as, every day, she put on the face that was needed to face her adoring public, and she took them to her heart as they took her to theirs – but that young woman was often lost in the middle of the crowds as the world looked on.

CHAPTER 8

ROS COWARD

'They've come out to see my wife,
they haven't come to see me.'

It's fair to say that the Royal Family is not the most emotionally literate clan that has ever walked the earth. When Diana arrived on the scene, here was someone completely different, who must have seemed harder to deal with. From what we know now, as Diana's mental distress increased, as she developed and lived with bulimia, and as she struggled with depression, it must have been a challenge for her husband to relate to her.

Diana developed bulimia pretty soon after she got married and it seems to have been brought on by the stress of being in the public eye and not having any real provision made for what she needed. Maybe from the beginning, she was a difficult prospect for them but that doesn't excuse the failure to guide and look after her. There is a history in Diana's family of anorexia and bulimia. Her sister, Sarah (who was once the love interest of Prince Charles) has said that she developed anorexia at one point. Frances Shand Kydd also confirmed the family history, when she told me, 'Diana was like me – when she was in a state, she would pick at her food. She was a picky girl, she couldn't eat.'

Diana became involved with an eating disorders charity in her final years and took the trouble to find out more about these conditions, which is interesting as it suggests that she was maybe in a place where she wanted to contextualise and analyse what had gone on in the past. Her comments in the Martin Bashir interview showed an incredible openness about her condition, an openness which other women would undoubtedly have found helpful, and which she appears to have passed down to her sons, particularly Harry. But both boys have picked up some of that – William clearly cares about mental health and that is an important legacy of her mothering. Both are young men who are prepared to talk about mental-health issues and describe how the loss of their mother affected them. That's an incredible change for Royals.

Referring to bulimia as a secret disease, Diana described how 'you inflict it upon yourself because your self-esteem is at a low ebb, and you don't think you are worthy or valuable.' She also talked about consciousness of her image, and of feeling when she was first exposed to the public scrutiny that she was still 'a fat chubby twenty-year-old of no interest.' Diana's body was a matter of public consumption and perhaps controlling that body was one of the only ways to take back a little power in a world where she felt powerless in so many ways. Towards the end of her life, she did go and see Susie Orbach, the author of *Fat is a Feminist Issue*. Orbach argued that women needed to be freed from the tyranny of eating and move away from seeing food as being linked to freedom or the lack of it. Did Diana relate to that message?

That period in the mid-1990s must have been terribly lonely for Diana. She was in the middle of all that attention in an iconic family, and struggling with many demons. Demons that so many ordinary women deal with. The gilded cage didn't protect Diana and she did very much become 'everywoman'. Her struggles covered many issues that many women could relate to – her weight, her exposure to the male gaze, her eating disorder, and her wishes: to be a modern mother, to parent differently, to have an independent *raison d'être*, to have a place in the world that she had earned by herself. It was almost what feminism was talking about at that moment. It had become a culturally transformative movement and what it stood for – women's independence and equality – was beginning to be embedded in our culture. Diana could have learned so much from it. Whether she did explore sexual politics, we may never know, but the fact that she met Orbach and worked with groups such as Relate would suggest that she had a growing awareness. When we look at Diana through that lens, she becomes rather significant as a symbol of a sociocultural movement in a particular era. But all the Royal Family saw was a young woman who wasn't acting in the way she should have been – in the 'proper' way.

Diana's popularity – and the way the public related to her struggles rather than condemned them – seemed to have provoked jealousy towards her from Charles himself. Some of the charities say that, at the very beginning, he was quite proud of her during an early visit to Wales and their initial public appearances, but that soon faded. The crowds went mad for her – they groaned when he walked on their side of the road and cheered when she did. When Charles said, 'They've come out to see my wife, they haven't come to see me,' no one knew the extent of that resentment and the envy which would grow from that comment.

The family couldn't understand what they would have considered to be unearned status. Again, there wasn't much support. The public love that Diana engendered wasn't something she could control, and she wasn't exploiting her popularity; in fact, in the early stages, she was almost cringing at it all. As she told Martin Bashir: 'The pressure on us both as a couple from the media was phenomenal.' She described how the crowds wanted her all the time, not Charles: 'I felt very uncomfortable with that, and felt it was unfair because I wanted to share.' Diana was naive at that stage, and she had an immature hope that everything would work out. I have spoken to many of her relatives and teachers, who all confirm that she had a crush on Charles and, as a young teenager, even had a picture of him on her wall. I think she probably entered into it all believing it could be a romantic relationship that worked as, from everything everyone has said, she was in love with him.

Charles was still in a relationship with Camilla during his engagement to Diana – he claims that he broke it off in the early part of the marriage but who knows? Clearly, from some quarters, there was an expectation that Diana would have no force, she would have no equal view on that ongoing liaison, and she would simply accept it – but there is evidence that she panicked upon discovering the extent of the relationship. This happened practically on the eve of the wedding when she discovered a bracelet Charles had had made for Camilla, engraved with the initials *F* and *G*, to signify their pet names for each other of Fred and Gladys.

When you think of how young Diana was when she was thrown into all of this, it is staggering. She was only nineteen when we all became aware of her, little more than a child. She had had a bit of real-world experience – unlike Kate Middleton, with whom she would later be compared – even if it was in the world of impoverished aristocracy. She had worked as a cleaner for her sister, and three days a week in a nursery as a kindergarten helper, but she was so young, with little education, few qualifications and a rather bereft childhood. She was privileged in many ways but deprived in others.

Some have compared Diana's uncomfortable position in the Royal Family with that of Princess Margaret, the Queen's wayward sister. But unlike Margaret, Diana had little sense of entitlement. She felt she had to earn her applause. In particular, Diana found the unearned adoration for her appearance problematic, she felt she had been commodified: 'You see yourself as a good product that sits on the shelf and sells well, and people make a lot of money.' She had been quite gauche when she married into the Royal Family and when she blossomed, it occurred when she was completely in the public eye, and at a time when women's bodies were being exposed to a whole new level of attention. It was a period when supermodels were becoming headline news. There was a heightened attention to women's style and clothing, as well as British fashion in particular – and suddenly, there was a young royal woman who embodied all of that, in terms of her looks, style, height and figure. Initially, that attention on her body was a factor in her eating disorder and she struggled to be seen in that same league.

In terms of her status, she felt she had to earn that too and this came through her rapid involvement in a huge number of charities. Princess Margaret had done that as well but, again, she didn't have quite the same approach. Diana did have an attempt at self-definition and that is why she is such a relatable figure – she was trying to define her place and her own interests, and she wasn't trying to have anything grand for herself. She never wanted the unquestioning kudos that some of the Royals enjoy. I feel there was both a sense that position had to be earned and that she was on a journey even before the relationship became so catastrophically bad. She would throw herself into things, such as becoming Patron of the Royal Association for Deaf people, which almost immediately became very important to her. She learned and became competent at sign language very quickly, taking it all seriously, and embraced the issues in depth rather than just turning up for a handshake. She might have self-deprecatingly called herself 'thick' on many occasions, but she was no such thing, even though she may have lacked academic qualifications.

That was all indicative of her personality. During the course of conducting many interviews, I discovered a great deal about her childhood, and it was clear that her caring nature and her compassion were there from her childhood. Several family members told me that it was instilled from an early age: her family held to an ethos of looking after the locals – both her parents believed in local charity and helping out. On top of that, Diana was a very compassionate child with an immense readiness to relate to people who needed help. She would go to the local care home and dance with the residents, she would readily engage with children and others from all walks of life well before she became a princess. There is a great deal of evidence to show that she had a natural gift for people – which is vastly different from traditional royal behaviour.

When Diana and Charles went to events and she was presented with flowers, she would get right down to the level of the people and talk to them, really engage with them. It was a very different type of engagement from the one people had with the Queen or any other Royal. People were thrilled that this very glamorous woman brought such a human touch. They gravitated towards her, wanting contact – and she allowed it. She would often insist on taking off her gloves before shaking hands with people as she wanted to feel them; she herself wanted that contact. That was there from the beginning and continued all the way through her life. There are some lovely pictures of her later on where she is touching children in her charities. Some of those children had lost limbs, in another picture she is seen touching a dying child's face with her hand. Diana just had that instinctive compassion and warmth, which made her a different entity from anyone previously seen in royal life before. She did seem different, and it was a new approach.

The public watched the evolution of Diana into a beautiful, caring woman, but behind the veil, she was doing what many women do – hiding a lot of what went on in private to conduct a public role. Only when Andrew Morton's book came out did so many faint rumours become known as fact. Many issues were finally addressed and many questions answered: her weight, the state of her relationship with Charles, his involvement with Camilla, and even the attempts Diana had made to take her own life. She put on an incredibly brave face.

She often said, 'Why don't they ever thank me for what I do?' and that feeling of desperation expressed itself through her bulimia, through the revelations about Charles's infidelity.

Yet she was still at the same time turning out in public and putting on a glamorous show. I can see why she felt she ought to be thanked for it but never was. In fact, as far as the accounts are available, some members of the Royal Family were baffled by and unsympathetic towards her mental illness – they didn't understand it and never wanted to address it. In particular, Prince Charles was very unsympathetic and just didn't get what it was about, thinking that she was quite crazy, particularly with regard to her cry for help when she flung herself down the stairs when pregnant with William.

Diana had very few people she could trust. Some have suggested that she had a relationship with one of her first bodyguards, Barry Mannakee. This is, of course, a rather popular trope in fiction, the relationship developing between the protected and the protector, the man who is looking at you all of the time, keeping you safe. In fact, there is no evidence that she did have this relationship, although she did become close to him. When he was dismissed from royal duty and was later killed in a motorcycle accident she was distraught. Her intimacy with people from 'outside the ranks' would have been absolute anathema to the Royal Family, just like so many baffling things she did.

Diana was an enigma for many people – whether for the public who loved her, or the Royal Family who were confused or enraged by her. Underlying it all, I feel, is that despite the wealth and indulgence of her life as a princess, she was living an existence which spoke to many women. Her husband was unfaithful. She had difficult in-laws. She was excluded from many things and only wheeled out when her presence was useful to others. She had difficult times during pregnancy. She had an eating disorder, depression, and a sense of never being accepted for who she was. She felt she was never encouraged; she was always expected to be something for other people. For so many women who were watching the soap opera of the monarchy unfold in front of their very eyes, Diana was the greatest character of all – and the most relatable.

CHAPTER 9

KEN WHARFE

'You should do something nice, Diana.
Why can't you do nice things?'

FOR 99.9 PER CENT of my time working with Diana, it was an extraordinary experience. I loved the opportunities my work gave me, but I couldn't wait to get back and see my own friends or just do something that was normal. It was all very pleasurable but so unreal. I was incredibly privileged to travel the world with her – it was an historical journey in many ways and a real art form in working on a security package not only in the UK but in many other parts of the world. Formulating those plans and putting them into practice, advising her at the same time, and being with somebody who made things work for so many different people was a life-changing combination.

When she decided to go solo, she was working for causes for women in Islamabad and then travelled to the Afghanistan/Pakistan border, to visit centres on the border of the refugee camp who provided prostheses for injured children during the Afghan War. She made a huge difference and she knew that. But I think the biggest example of her campaigning power came when she became involved in AIDS awareness in the mid-1980s.

Diana would visit the Queen on a fairly regular basis, once a fortnight, usually on a Wednesday or a Thursday, to have tea for forty minutes or so. I'd drive her down, go through the Garden Gate as you look at Buckingham Palace on the right-hand side, then park under a tree and read a paper while she had a nice time with the Queen; these were happy visits but one day she came out crying. I asked her what was wrong.

As I told the High Court at Diana's inquest, the Princess was distressed after she said that the Queen had voiced her disapproval of Diana's involvement with AIDS charities, wanting her to concentrate on something more pleasant.

Now, it has to be said that this was not a very popular subject at the time. HIV and AIDS were known as the 'Gay Plague' and very few people wanted to be associated with any of it. Diana was different. She was raising awareness and breaking down barriers.

Diana was seriously upset by that response from Her Majesty – and she was up against that kind of thing from other royal figures too. Her maternal grandmother, Ruth, Lady Fermoy, the Queen Mother's lady-in-waiting and a woman of her vintage, was an extraordinary person. In my opinion she was not very nice at all – very much in the camp of old-school royalty, very powerful, very class conscious, and also, in my opinion, instrumental in putting forward Diana as a candidate for the Prince of Wales in the late 1970s. One day, Diana had been to see a friend at her favourite restaurant San Lorenzo and came back to Kensington Palace

Above left: The Hon, Diana Spencer, as she then was, as a toddler.

Above right: Diana with her brother younger brother Charles, now Lord Spencer.

Below: Early press attention for the Prince of Wales's fiancée: Lady Diana Spencer outside the apartment block in Earl's Court where she lived before her marriage, November 1980.

Above: The marriage of the Prince and Princess of Wales at St Paul's Cathedral, 29 July 1981 – Diana had just turned nineteen.

Below: Two photographs of Charles and Diana on honeymoon by the River Dee, on the Queen's Balmoral Estate in Aberdeenshire, August 1981.

Above: An unwitting Diana with Camilla Parker Bowles at Ludlow Races in 1980, before the former's marriage. Prince Charles was competing in the Amateur Riders' Handicap Steeplechase; Camilla was still married to Andrew Parker Bowles.

Left: The Prince and Princess of Wales with their newborn son, Prince William, on the steps of St Mary's Hospital, London, June 1982.

Above: 'The heir and the spare': just over three years after William's birth, the couple leave the hospital's Lindo Wing with Prince Harry, September 1984.

Below: Diana with Harry and Charles with William on board the Royal Yacht, HMY *Britannia*, during their visit to Venice, May 1985.

Above left: Diana talking to Elton John (centre) and George Michael at the Feed the World Live Aid concert at Wembley, July 1985. In a sad irony, Elton John would perform a rewritten version of his 'Candle in the Wind' at Diana's funeral twelve years later.

Above right: Diana and her police protection officer, Ken Wharfe, shelter beneath an umbrella during a visit to flood victims in Camarthen, Wales, October 1987.

Below: April 1992: Ken exiting the Princess's car to deal with a demonstrator as she arrives at the shipyard in Barrow-in-Furness for the naming ceremony of HMS *Vanguard*, Britain's first Trident nuclear submarine,

Above: Diana with Ken in Brazil, April 1991. She is wearing one of the two dresses she bought from her friend Kanga Tryon's shop for £3,500 each – prompting Ken's remark about pasta . . .

Below left: Diana and and a vigilant Ken Wharfe during a visit to Munster, Germany, in June 1991.

Below right: Diana and Ken arriving at an AIDS information kiosk in the Latin quarter of Paris in November 1992. Her work for AIDS awareness did much to counter the stigma then surrounding the disease.

Left: Diana with William and Harry in school uniform on Harry's first day at Wetherby Prep School in September 1989 – she was always a hands-on mother to the boys, often undertaking the school run.

Below: Barefoot princess: Diana taking part in the mothers' race during Harry's school sports day, June 1991.

Above: Diana greets her sons on board *Britannia* in Toronto, when the boys joined their parents for an official visit to Canada, 23 October 1991.

Right: Diana was always keen that her sons should be able to take part in 'ordinary' activities, rather than staying within the royal bubble. With William and Harry at Thorpe Park, south-west of London, in April 1993.

Above: Diana leaves Lech in Austria on learning of the death of her father in March 1992. Ken (out of shot in the front passenger seat) persuaded her to allow the Prince of Wales to travel back to England with her, which at first she had adamantly opposed.

Below: Flanked by William and Harry, Diana attends the Heads of State VE Day Remembrance Service in Hyde Park, 7 May 1995.

wearing a pair of leather culottes. Who should be standing at the door, for some reason, but Ruth Fermoy?

The older woman looked at Diana with a steely-eyed stare and exclaimed, 'Look at you! Look at you! You look like a strumpet!'

I don't think Diana knew what a strumpet was. 'What do you mean?' she asked, looking down at her outfit.

'Just look at them! There is nothing royal about those!'

That was what she was up against – everyone but her mother, sister and brother were loyal to the Prince of Wales; even her brother-in-law and sister Jane found it incredibly difficult because they were so close to the Queen. They were certainly not outspoken in defence of Diana as it would offend the Prince and the Queen. In that sense, even then, as Diana told me, she felt she was being marginalised by her own family. There was no way Ruth Fermoy would protect her granddaughter, she would have been too far up the scale of royal connections to come out and defend what she had decided was indefensible. The Prince of Wales mattered much more.

Diana was committed to her AIDS campaign work, often alongside her friend Elton John. Before her run-in with the Queen, we had already been visiting the London Lighthouse and other hospices on a fairly regular basis, and I must say these visits were quite an eye-opener. I saw people very close to death and it was Diana's idea that we all needed to fight for a cure. She knew that one of the things she was very good at was charging £1,000 for a ticket or selling off one of her mantel clocks for £10,000. She was shrewd in that sense, and she used that shrewdness to really generate donations. Her work with AIDS charities was instrumental in eventually funding research for a cure, as she had wanted.

Seeing and being alongside Diana, working with these charities, made me realise there was a much bigger side to the story. I could understand how she felt as I remember one journalist calling her 'The Goddess of Sodomy', because of this fear, opposition and hatred towards the AIDS crisis. It wasn't just those charities which opened my eyes – I was able to sit in on conferences such as those with Relate and that was an education for me. I was very fortunate to have that access.

Nothing is perfect in this industry. There is no such thing as total security unless you put forty feet of razor wire on top of the Palace walls and put the Queen in a metal box – even then she might suffer from heat exhaustion – but Diana often didn't see why she should be curtailed. To be perfectly honest, I often agreed with her and went out of my way to give her the freedom she so desperately craved.

I remember once, in the mid-1980s, coming back from my aunt's house in Dorset, and Diana greeted me with, 'Have you had a good weekend?'

'Yes, it was lovely, thanks – I saw my aunt and went for a lovely walk on Studland Beach in Dorset.'

'You're so lucky, Ken. I can't do that. They won't let me.'

'Who are "they"?'

'You. You wouldn't let me do it.'

'Well, you've never asked. If you want to do it, we can do it.'

'What? You'll take all your men and follow me? I can't be doing with that.'

'Hang on a minute,' I replied. 'You're assuming a lot. Ask me and we'll see what we can do.'

She thought about it, she did ask, and we decided to go that Thursday.

'We leave here at 7.30 a.m. – don't say anything to anybody. We'll take the Ford Mondeo, not the Jaguar.'

The Mondeo was two-tone red with a black roof – hardly royal! We drove down to Poole Harbour and got on the chain ferry, with Diana wearing a leather jacket given to her by Michael Jackson. People were staring at her, and I'm sure they must have been thinking, 'God, she looks really like Diana, doesn't she?' We got off at the other side and parked, I gave her a radio and she disappeared off along the beach. That was it. I told her to let me know if there was a problem. After about an hour, the phone crackled into life, and I could hear Diana laughing.

'What's up?'

'Oh, you didn't tell me about the nudist beach, Ken!' she giggled. She'd stumbled across a dozen septuagenarian males in their birthday suits who had no clue who this woman in a Michael Jackson jacket was, and neither were they interested! We met up and had some breakfast, went to Corfe Castle and visited the National Trust shop – no one was any the wiser.

'There you are – anything is possible,' I told her when we got back to London. This is where Diana was so different. No one else would have done that. She brought out a human side in me in my job and I genuinely thank the Department and the Waleses for opening me up to that.

Diana was optimistic about her leading role in society, once she had left Charles and, having spoken to Prime Ministers John Major and then Tony Blair, they both apparently – according to her – said, 'We could use you in an ambassadorial role given your experience in the charitable field.' I think she firmly believed that would happen – but of course, it did not. In fact, none of the notions dangled in front of her materialised. During 1994–95, apart from her landmine journey, there was no real work at all and she was personally without security as she had declined the protection of Scotland Yard.

Diana's loyalty to the Queen could not be faulted but, I am absolutely certain that, once it had been noted that she had abandoned the security (first with me in October 1993, then the entire security content two months later), the Queen could have insisted that she retain it. Had she done that, in my view, Diana would have accepted it. Had that been the case, she'd still be alive.

The year 1993 was, to put it mildly, a difficult one for Diana. In 1992, John Major had announced in Parliament that she and the Prince of Wales were going to separate. Diana knew, the Prince of Wales knew, and I think the Government knew that this was the beginning of the end and divorce would inevitably follow. By 1993, she wasn't the Diana I had known in the previous six years. In her place was a very troubled woman, clearly uncertain as to where her own life was going, and bitter that any chance of a reconciliation had gone. The latter was largely due to the fateful meeting she had with Camilla in 1989 at a party in Richmond. The Prince had tried to persuade her not to attend the 'ghastly' event but Diana persisted, contrary to what everyone expected. Diana, by her own admission, was on edge. She gave Camilla a formal handshake rather than a kiss, and, during the party when she realised that her husband and his mistress had disappeared, began searching for them. Upon arrival at the house, once I was happy with the security, I told Diana I would be in the kitchen, should she need me. Within an hour I heard my name being called.

It was Diana. I found her in the corridor, distressed and clearly unhappy.

'What's the matter?' I asked.

'I can't find my husband and cannot see Camilla – I want you to try and find them with me.'

We walked with pace to the basement of the house and there, sat on a small two-seater sofa, was the Prince and Camilla engaged in conversation. With extraordinary confidence Diana walked towards Camilla and said, 'Camilla, I would just like you to know that I know exactly what's going on.'

She said, 'I don't know what you're talking about.'

Diana replied, 'I know what's going on between you and Charles, and I just want you to know that.'

Camilla responded, 'You've got everything you've ever wanted. You've got all the men in the world falling in love with you, you've got two wonderful boys, what more do you want?'

'I want my husband,' Diana said. 'Don't treat me like an idiot.'

What followed that was most definitely the beginning of the end.

I think the hardest element was towards the end in 1993, after her separation from Charles the previous year. That was a real turning point for Diana as she had decided that she was out of there. She really meant that – she just needed to time it and make her exit as clever as possible, and I do think that she started to wind down, professionally and mentally. I rather wonder about the effect Martin Bashir and his famous interview had – even before she first met him in 1994, she firmly believed that people were against her. She was certainly slightly paranoid about being bugged, but there was no basis for that as far as I could see as I had arranged for government services to debug her room, and they found nothing.

Clearly, she was of a mindset that people were against her for whatever reason. She always believed that the 'B Team' were out to get her – and perhaps on reflection there might be an element of truth in that, given the Prince of Wales's position and the size and strength of his entourage. In 1993, she was clearly on the way out. No one would have expected that she would go at the end of that year, and it made life very difficult for me.

During a holiday in the Caribbean towards the end of my time with her, with William and Harry, Diana was difficult and wouldn't play ball with anyone. When we came back, we went almost immediately to Ludgrove School, to see William play football. She drove down in her green Jaguar, although I had a back-up crew in the distance, which she accepted as the rule. On the way, Diana said to me, 'I'm not speaking to any parents, Ken.'

'That's fine – do what you like,' I replied.

'No, I'm just going to annoy William.'

'What do you want to do that for?'

'I'll do what I want,' she retorted, as she so often did.

'I know you'll do what you want, but why? I'm asking you, why? He isn't going to like his mother, is he, when all of the others are on the touchline being supportive and you just want to annoy him? Not a good idea, Ma'am. He isn't going to like that, it will be embarrassing for him.'

'I'll do what I want, Ken,' she repeated.

'Fine.'

We arrived and she totally ignored the headmaster. All of the dutiful parents were hoping for a glimpse, a handshake or a chat with the Princess of Wales but they were seriously out of luck that day. William was in goal. Diana immediately went around the back of the goalmouth and, as soon as the match began, started ridiculing him about his spindly white legs.

I stood at a discreet distance but could hear every insult.

'You've got horrible legs,' she told him.

'Oh, for God's sake, go away, Mummy,' he said. 'You're making me so embarrassed!'

'Look,' I implored her, 'there's your answer. There's how you're making him feel.'

'I don't need you to tell me that, Ken.'

'I *am* telling you! You're making the kid's life purgatory in front of his mates – that's the last thing he needs! You should really stop it.'

I was quite open in my condemnation that day as I didn't like what I was seeing. Yes, I could have walked away from it, but I felt compelled to say something.

She eventually gave up, the game ended and we drove back to London. As we got near to Kensington High Street, with me driving this time, she declared, 'I need some shopping. Just park here.'

'Sorry?'

'Park the car, Ken. I want to go to Tower Records.'

'No, I'm sorry, I can't just park here. Let's go back to Kensington Palace and I can park there.'

'No, I don't want that.'

'Then we're not parking the car here.'

I didn't want an argument so I drove into Kensington Palace Gardens, and spoke with the armed police officer outside the Israeli Embassy and asked for his permission to park. He recognised Diana of course, and replied with a dutiful, 'Not a problem.'

Diana opened the door and ran off up towards Kensington

Palace Gardens. *I'm not running after you*, I thought. I left the car and walked at a perfectly normal pace after her. The armed Embassy policeman must have wondered what sort of protection I was providing, given that my royal charge had just bolted away from me! Knowing that she wanted to buy some CDs, I went directly to the shop – Tower Records in Kensington High Street – and stood outside. Diana eventually came out with a batch of CDs.

'Have you got forty pounds?' she asked, as if nothing else had happened.

'Sure.'

I gave her the money, she went back to pay for them and we walked back to the car. That was the point when I decided, this is probably the right time to leave. It took me about a week to sort it out. I simply felt that I couldn't keep her safe any longer as her behaviour was so erratic. I actually felt that my presence was compromising her security. That very act at the end, running up Kensington Palace Gardens, was the tipping point. I wasn't thinking for one moment that an assassin was going to kill her, but she could have fallen over, she could have been run over, and had that been the case, it would have been my responsibility and I would have carried the blame. Leaving was the right thing to do, but I didn't know at that point that she would completely pull out of all security cover weeks later – and that would ultimately lead to her death. No one could have predicted that.

When we see what has gone on with Harry and Meghan with regards to security, it can feel as if history is repeating itself. If Harry and Meghan had stayed in the United Kingdom, there wouldn't be a problem as they would have that security detail which seems so contentious to them. The very fact that they are now domiciled in

America means that things have changed. They no longer represent the Royal Family – as the Queen made quite clear when Harry thought that he might be able to juggle six months in London with six months somewhere else. The Royals were never going to buy that option. I knew then that the British Government and Scotland Yard were unlikely to fund an expensive security package because the taxpayer wouldn't buy it. When Harry and Meghan withdrew their services, their popularity plummeted and, instead of having a very positive following from within the British public, they were seen in a different light. There is no doubt about it, Harry was the number one celebrity in the eyes of the public, he was part of the future of the British monarchy, and he was Diana's son. That has all been thrown away – at least temporarily.

Harry now employs private security in America and I have a fairly good idea what that's like. They'll certainly keep them alive, but the subtleties of that protection will be so different from those we have in this country. He knows that. He says that when he comes back to the United Kingdom, he'll need Scotland Yard protection. Well, that is purely dependent on the risk factor. If there is a serious threat against his life, then they would probably advise him not to come anyway. He wants that level and show of security because he feels he's entitled to it, but sadly for him it won't happen just because he demands it – despite his offer to pay for security while in the UK; that is not how the Home Office works. I don't think he's getting a raw deal – he's just not getting what he wants. Everyone understands why he left and there is a great deal of sympathy for that, but when you start laying down demands from a foreign land – that, quite rightly, doesn't go down too well with the British people.

CHAPTER 10

ROS COWARD

'There were three of us in this marriage
so it was a bit crowded.'

IT'S THE QUOTE everyone remembers. When Diana told
Martin Bashir in the stunning *Panorama* interview, broadcast
in November 1995, 'There were three of us in this marriage so it
was a bit crowded,' the effect was astonishing. It was an incredible
moment where she put her finger on what had been going on in
her life and really communicated it to the general public in a way
that they completely understood. The wife of the future King was
telling the world that he was in a relationship with another woman.
It was absolute dynamite.

Those are probably Diana's own words. I'd be extremely
surprised if the comment wasn't her personal formulation as it was
very typical of her own manner of speaking. She had this wit and
sharpness and seemed to be able to find the right words for things,
despite regarding herself as not highly educated. I think it absolutely
came straight from her heart, and described what she felt about the

marriage, but it also reached out and spoke to a lot of women. For all the framing of the Bashir interview and the questions behind it, that was a moment where it was Diana herself talking to the public, where they heard her own words from her own mouth for the first time. There had been rumours and gossip flying around for years that Charles had carried on his relationship with Camilla Parker Bowles right from the start of his time with Diana, and even suggestions that her marriage didn't really have a chance.

The quote summed up the whole story from the very beginning. Although the public wanted to believe in the fairy tale, from the moment when Diana became engaged to Prince Charles and introduced to the public, there was always the question in their mind that, however delightful it all seemed, was he truly in love with her the way she seemed to be with him? There was that famous first interview when the engagement was announced and Alastair Burnet asked Charles, 'Are you very much in love, Sir?' Charles replied, 'Oh yes … whatever love means.' A suspicion was planted that he didn't have a wholehearted commitment to his young bride-to-be and this bewildered the public. Diana was everything *they* wanted and yet he already seemed to be cynical about their connection.

It may be hard to recall but Charles was actually known at the time as a bit of a Casanova. He'd been associated with all sorts of women, relationships had been talked about in the press, and one of them was even with Diana's sister, Sarah. She was a serious contender according to commentators but she declared herself that she wasn't in love with him and it wasn't going to happen. He was represented as a dashing prince about town and there was enormous interest when he decided to settle down with this young woman who, allegedly, was looked on favourably by the Queen Mother as eminently suitable breeding stock.

Camilla was barely known about at that time, although Charles's relationship with her was ongoing. But from the beginning, Diana became aware of this woman's presence and was taken aback by the way Camilla seemed to assume some kind of control between the two of them. The older woman wanted to become friendly, to tell the new ingénue what to do, and to give her guidance, whereas Diana didn't understand the intimacy between her and Charles – including the exchange of the infamous Fred and Gladys bracelets just before their wedding, their pet names for each other, the initials intertwined.

Few people know the details of whether or not Charles did give up Camilla at any point during their marriage, but by the time Diana came to speak to Andrew Morton for his book, *Diana: Her True Story* (republished after her death with '*In Her Own Words*' added to the title), she was desperate to speak out about her struggle with a marriage where she felt she didn't really have a chance – even though by then she was known to have had some of her own dalliances. Morton has stated that he believes one of her motivations for her involvement in the book was that she didn't want to be blamed for having these relationships herself and wanted people to understand what had been going on in the marriage so far.

Of course, Morton didn't name Camilla, he didn't expose the details of the relationship even though Diana wanted that to be part of the material. They took the decision simply to refer to it as a 'close friendship' on many occasions in the text. In a later edition of the book, Morton himself said that he persuaded and reassured

Diana that a repeated nuanced comment like that would allow people to draw their own conclusions. She accepted that in the end. The important part of that is 'Charles and his lady' did dominate what was going on in the marriage and was clearly a massive part of the disintegration of the relationship – Diana had been left on her own with very little guidance from the start and pretty much always had a suspicion that Charles, when he wasn't there, was with Camilla.

When Diana finally formulated it as 'three of us in this marriage', there was a surge of public support for her, particularly among women. They saw her as having had this relationship hanging over all of her attempts to make the marriage work. Even though she admitted to the depth of her feelings for James Hewitt, what the public heard was her distress that Charles and Camilla's affair had doomed her relationship. Whether she had been manipulated or not to talk more openly than some thought wise, the fact is that in baring her soul the public related to her. They felt it explained a lot – who wouldn't react like that?

We didn't know terms like 'gaslighting' and 'ghosting' then, but this is what Diana described. Schedules were shifted to allow Charles to use different houses to meet Camilla, with friends colluding in the deceit and also telling Diana that she was paranoid and imagining things. She wasn't paranoid about this at all, it was true and many women who have experienced betrayal could relate to that. Women are constantly told: You're imagining things, you're making up an affair, you're seeing things that aren't there, and for this to be happening to the Princess of Wales made her more relatable than ever. Allegations of mental-health issues have been thrown at women for ever. Hysteria, for example, was a term originally implying a woman's disorder. The word derived from the Greek for uterus (*utera*). Diana certainly suffered all her life from accusations of excessive emotionality and especially of paranoia; indeed, the issue of her 'paranoia' is one of the enduring themes of her life. Yet with Camilla, the evidence was there.

There was a curious way in which things Diana worried about sometimes came to pass. She was pretty 'paranoid' or suffered heightened anxiety about her safety and her security. Disgracefully, Martin Bashir exploited these fears when he secured the interview with her, having inflamed ideas that her most loyal staff were in fact spying on her and conspiring against her.

When Charles confessed to his adultery with Camilla, in a TV interview with Jonathan Dimbleby in 1994, he used the most unfortunate phrasing:

Dimbleby asked, 'Do you wish it would go away?'

Charles replied, 'Of course I wish it would go away. Of course I wish it could be over and done with.'

If you take that at face value, Charles is simply saying relationships go wrong and that his has gone wrong, and he regrets it, wishing that it hadn't. But saying these things in a rather bleak tone of voice made Diana think that he really did wish her to go away.

Charles didn't initially want to mention his adultery in the documentary presented by Jonathan Dimbleby that preceded Diana's own interview, and which doubtless contributed to her desire to have her say. It was Dimbleby who persuaded him that it would be done in a sympathetic context which would make people understand him better. It didn't. After it was broadcast, *The Sun* took a snap poll of its readers, asking: Is Charles fit to be King? Two thirds said 'no.' There has been a long journey to rehabilitation of Charles and acceptance of Camilla since she loomed over Diana's life as this third presence in the marriage. It is clear from her own interview that Diana clearly did not think it was possible that Camilla and Charles would be able to marry and that if he lived with her, he could never become king. And it was, for a long time, seen as unlikely that Camilla could be rehabilitated in the public eye. But after a concerted effort by various people including Mark Bolland, Deputy Private Secretary to the Prince of Wales, Camilla has married Charles and is now seen by his side at public engagements. Time has passed, and, to some extent as she is recognised as the consort of Charles, this has increased her popularity. A narrative has emerged which sees Camilla as loyal, Charles's prop in life, the companion he should always have had. William at least seems to accept her as a person with a role in his father's life. But the affair left a residue of feeling among some of the population that neither she nor Charles are fit to be King and Queen Consort.

History has introduced a level of indifference to Camilla's existence but if you scratch beneath the surface and start retelling the story of Diana, it reawakens. Some embarrassing, even toe-curling revelations are part of the story of the affair. There was the famous leaked telephone conversation in which Charles says that he wishes he could be Camilla's tampon. It was the most uncomfortable thing to listen to or imagine a member of the Royal Family (or indeed anyone) saying. But there was another significant moment in that conversation. When Camilla says, 'I've never achieved anything', Charles replies, 'Your greatest achievement is to have loved me.'

These words brought into focus the difference between Diana and Camilla. In a nutshell, Diana was struggling to be a sort of equal with Charles – not trying to have a career by any means but struggling to have some parity in their marriage in a way that is seen as perfectly normal with most couples. She had a sense of modernity and equality that sharply contrasted with Camilla's status. Camilla's role was very passive, dutiful, making no demands, whereas Diana had all the expectations of a modern marriage. Diana anticipated being within a partnership, doing things together with her husband, and was very put out when she realised what was happening.

One of the many charities Diana was involved with was Relate, which offers marriage counselling. Diana often talked openly to organisers and groups at the charities, and apparently was very forthcoming and open about her issues, as well as showing great empathy for others. She established many friendships and contacts at those groups, and obviously told people that she was desperately unhappy, attending several of the groups and talking to them openly. Similar conversations took place at many other different charities, where she would talk about her eating disorder, self-harming, suicide attempts, and mental health, which left a lot of people realising that she was unhappy and struggling to come to terms with the hand she'd been dealt.

Such was Diana's character that she was unable to bottle things up, and this was probably a significant contributing factor in her alienation from the Royal Family. Diana's character was such that she spoke what was on her mind and didn't try to repress her emotions. She never would have, wherever she'd landed in life. Everyone would probably agree that the Royal Family is repressed, and that they don't wear their hearts on their sleeves, and it's likely they were somewhat contemptuous of Diana speaking out in that way. Diana's openness came naturally to her and extended to remarks she made openly critical of the Royal Family. 'The way they bring up children is weird,' she once said, making it clear that she didn't want the boys' upbringing to be like that. She wanted them to be in touch with their feelings and with ordinary life outside the Royal Family, seeing how the other half lived.

After the Bashir interview, the Queen was reported as saying, 'There will never be a reconciliation now, they'd better just get divorced.' It is also claimed that she said that what Diana did was 'quite dreadful'. I'm sure that, in their eyes, Diana's behaviour was so far beyond the bounds of what they consider acceptable that she must have seemed almost mad.

Now that Charles and Camilla are married the contrasts between the two women's expectations of relationships are there to see. Diana was a young woman struggling to achieve an equal partnership, Camilla represents a traditional patriarchal consort who seems never to complain or assert herself.

Camilla has her house in Wiltshire, and it is said that she and Charles certainly don't spend every minute together. But they are clearly comfortable with each other. Statements from Charles are loving, as was seen in the recent announcement that the Queen made, saying that Camilla should be accepted as Queen Consort. There was a high price paid for this relationship, namely Diana's mental well-being, so there is a lot depending on it being seen as stable and worth the suffering.

Is it time to forget about Diana's grievance against the treatment she received in her marriage? Now that Camilla and Charles are married, and he obviously loves and leans on Camilla – as was very apparent at the Queen's Platinum Jubilee – is it time for everyone to move on? Maybe. But anyone who recalls Diana's story will realise that the very public disintegration of her marriage, her treatment by the establishment and her tragic death added up to more than just the story of three people in a marriage. It was a story that ripped the veil off royal behaviour and raised questions about the suitability of these people and their fitness for office.

CHAPTER 11

KEN WHARFE

'I don't go by the rule book. I lead from the heart, not the head.'

DIANA WAS VERY keen at one point, influenced by Fergie, to have a female member of staff on her team. I thought that was a good idea and managed to get Carol Quirk, who was a friend of mine in the Close Protection Office. Unfortunately, she didn't last very long.

Diana used to go to a gym out in Hounslow and one day told Carol that she was off there for a session. Carol dressed accordingly – dressed down, as it were, in a tracksuit, but Diana turned up in a pin-striped suit with her hair done and in full make-up.

'Oh, I thought we were going to the gym?' said Carol.

'We are, but I have to go straight to the office afterwards,' Diana told her. That put Carol in a complete spin because she would then have to turn up at St James's Palace in jogging bottoms and a sweatshirt. It seemed rather naughty of Diana. I had a discussion about it, and reminded her that it was best all round for her to let us know her plans. She accepted that, but it was a rather difficult conversation.

About two weeks later, Diana said to me, 'I think people are taking photographs of me at the gym.'

'What makes you think that?'

'I just think they are. Can you go and have a word with the man who runs the place?'

'Well, I could do, but it would help me if you can say why you think photographs are being taken, otherwise I'm going in completely blind just on your hunch, which doesn't really make sense. How do you know it's happening?'

'I can't really tell you.'

'That's not fair, is it? Why can't you?'

'I just can't.'

'So, does that mean you *know* they're being taken or that you *knew*, because there's a slightly different implication.'

'No, I *know* they have.'

I backed off a bit on the questioning and called the gym manager, an Australian guy called Bryce Taylor.

'I need to speak to you.'

'What about, mate?'

'Some photographs.'

'Oh, I'm not here after tomorrow.'

'That's fine – I'll come over now.'

I drove there immediately, and he was a nervous wreck. There was a gantry that went around the gym, and I checked it. I couldn't see any evidence of cameras, but there was every opportunity he could have taken photographs from his room, had he wanted to. He was adamant that he had done no such thing, but I didn't believe him. I could see on his face that he was lying but I had no evidence. Something certainly didn't sit right with me.

I said to Diana afterwards, 'I have no evidence of photographs.'

'I know there are some.'

'Well, I don't because I haven't seen any. Let's leave it at that.'

A day later, I got a phone call from Lord Mishcon, Diana's lawyer.

'Can you come and see me, Inspector?' he asked.

'About what, Sir?'

'These photographs …'

'Well, I know that the Princess has mentioned the possibility of photographs being taken of her whilst exercising, but I haven't seen any. Have you?'

'No.'

'Well, with due respect, why would I come to see you? You don't know and I don't know – the one person who does know is for some reason reluctant to reveal her source of information.'

'I would be grateful, Inspector, if you would come and see me.'

I did. There was this elderly man sitting at his lawyer's desk, presumably no wiser than me about the photographs.

'I'd like to take a statement from you about these photographs.'

'Lord Mishcon, firstly I'm not prepared to give a statement until I have the authorisation from the Commissioner of Police. Secondly, I'm sorry, but what is the point of me giving you a statement about something I know nothing about? I've been to the gym, I've spoken to Bryce Taylor, there was nothing to suggest to me anything untoward happened.'

I had to rely here on evidence, not gut feeling, and at that point I had no evidence to suggest that any such photographs existed.

'Well, the whole point is, once we have your statement, we can apply for an injunction, should any newspapers print the photographs.'

I stared at him. 'I'm finding this very difficult, Sir. If a newspaper has these photographs, they'll print them whatever happens. They may very well be with an editor somewhere as we're speaking. By the time you get an injunction, it would be too late anyway.'

The Royals wouldn't ordinarily go for injunctions, but they would take legal advice. It was in the interests of top legal companies to have them on their list of clients but it was strange that someone as senior as Mishcon would get involved in this.

I finally got authority to make a statement, not that I had much to say. The following weekend, the front page of the *Sunday Mirror* had pictures of Diana, taken some weeks earlier, working out at the gym wearing make-up – around the time Carol had been involved. The actual source of the information to Diana was that, apparently, Taylor had given the negatives to someone who had worked in his gym, who just so happened to be a part-time hairdresser. He was clipping away one day when it just so happened a lady-in-waiting at Buckingham Palace heard his comments to someone else, and it eventually drip-fed its way back to Diana.

Bryce Taylor went back to Australia and Diana's legal action against Mirror Group Newspapers ended when a deal was done whereby the latter issued a public apology to her; it was also rumoured to have paid her legal costs and made a donation to one of her charities. It all ended rather weirdly. I have never understood this whole thing. Why did Diana go to that gym that morning dressed as she did with Carol Quirk? The photographs certainly showed her not in the normal gym mode you would expect of someone working out. She was perfectly made-up and very well-presented. To me, it was a story that was never satisfactorily resolved, and Diana was very closed-off about it, she wouldn't take it any further. Had she been told in confidence not to say anything? Did she think it could be resolved behind the scenes? There was no pecuniary advantage in it for Diana. The only thing that could come out of it were pictures of her looking good while she worked out in a gymnasium. She was vain, as we all are, and she did get annoyed when there were bad photographs of her. She could very well have been involved in all of this. When I went and looked at where she worked out, above her was a recess – perhaps a light fitting – which could have held a camera. Whether Diana was complicit with the taking of these photographs remains a mystery. I knew Taylor was lying but had no evidence to support Diana's fears – I suspect that Taylor dismantled whatever was in the roof as soon as I left.

I've never got to the bottom of that.

Carol had to go after that incident – there was no chemistry, which was a shame, and Diana never asked for another female officer. She related better to men and definitely preferred their company. Her girlfriends were fairly easy-going. I don't think they ever gave her a rough time, although she did fall out with two of them on their last skiing trip in the wake of her being given advice that she didn't want to hear.

As we reflect on Diana's enduring legacy, twenty-five years after her death, we cannot help but look into the more unedifying details of royal life – and is there anything more unedifying than the George Smith case, the resultant Peat Report and the behaviour of Diana's former butler, Paul Burrell?

The Peat Report by Sir Michael Peat and Edmund Lawson QC is an absolutely vital document for anyone who wants to attempt some understanding of what was going on at the Palace during the final years of Diana's life there. It looked into allegations made by the under-butler George Smith in 1996. Smith claimed that he had been raped by a member of the Kensington Palace staff, but he himself sadly died after the investigation had been completed, so any picture we have is an incomplete one.

A quick recap of the incident is that George Smith was late in taking breakfast to the Prince of Wales one morning. He claimed that when he took the tray to Charles, he saw him in a compromising situation with another servant, an allegation publicly denied on behalf of Charles at the time by his private secretary, Sir Michael Peat. Smith also said that he had been raped by a royal servant.

George Smith had been seconded to the Royal Household from the Welsh Guards and then 'bought out' by the Prince of Wales to take up permanent employment as a travelling orderly. I firmly believe that Smith was an honest man. Presumably, the Prince of Wales did too, or he would not have given him a permanent post once he had left the Army, and yet, no one believed his allegation when it was made – it appeared that they just wanted it to go away. Fearful of the story breaking in the media, lawyers for the Prince of Wales and senior household staff worked furiously to resolve the issue. The Prince of Wales's police officer, Chief Superintendent Trimming, would have been in no doubt about how serious this allegation was, and he would also have been privy to the details of the allegation. In my view Trimming had a duty to inform the police outside of royal palaces for an investigation to take place and assist Smith in the process immediately the allegation was known – but this never happened. The household set about destroying Smith's alleged story of events as 'fantasy'.

Diana heard the story in 1996, and set out on a journey to prove to herself that what George Smith had said was true. There were very few people left at Kensington Palace by then, the staff weren't well known to her, and she took it on herself to go with Victoria Mendham, who in my time would have been known as a lady clerk. Mendham was a lovely woman with a well-privileged background, and she looked the part. That was all Diana had, that was her artillery. Victoria was someone who would go anywhere with her, so off they went – twice – to see George Smith at The Priory.

In short, when George Smith made the allegation of being raped, to the office of the Prince of Wales, 'they' were very keen to brush this under the carpet. Lawyers from the Royal Household were placed in a very difficult position when this allegation came to light, given the seriousness of it, so whether it was true or not is almost irrelevant. The first port of call was that the allegation should have immediately gone to the police outside of the Palace, not the police *within* the Palace, to be investigated. They had foolishly not accounted for Diana stepping in several years later. The Princess desperately wanted to try and find out what had gone on, and she made huge steps towards that. However, the rest of us will never know as Smith is dead and, effectively, the matter is closed.

In summary, we are faced with two issues – the first, that the Prince of Wales and members of his household became aware that George Smith, who was then employed as a valet, had alleged that in 1989, he had been the victim of homosexual rape by another employee who was still a member of the household.

The second is that Diana then tape-recorded Smith's story while visiting him in The Priory.

It is part of Diana's legacy, although perhaps not a nice part, that she would have been somewhat excited by this mystery. It shows part of her character that she would have been rather thrilled. The rape was too big an issue for Diana not to get her teeth into, especially as there wasn't a great deal of royal business going on in her life and she could devote a lot of her time to becoming her own private detective. She said in the Martin Bashir interview that she didn't think her husband was fit to be king, and I think part of this was not just related to his adultery. I guess those tapes could have fuelled this belief.

All of this raises some very pertinent questions. For me, one of the main ones is: Who did George Smith speak to for this information to be known in the first place, and why was it not acted upon when the allegation of rape was made in 1995? Any such claim of rape should have been reported to the police for investigation. The report says that the allegations by Smith were first made in late 1995, to a fellow employee and also to Diana – which is rather odd given that, at the very beginning of his report, Peat says that Smith had alleged he had been raped in 1989.

In 1996 George Smith repeated his allegations to Hounslow Police but, after some equivocation, decided not to pursue the matter. The rape allegation then lay dormant until 2001 when, in connection with the proceedings against Burrell, Lady Sarah McCorquodale (Diana's sister) told police of having found, after the Princess's death, a sensitive tape recording, which had been suggested to have contained the recordings of Smith's allegations to Diana. She recalled entrusting the tape to Paul Burrell for safekeeping – which he denied. To this day, no such tape has been found. The tape had been placed in a mahogany box on Diana's desk, a box which she had said contained the 'Crown Jewels', many personal items including letters between her and James Hewitt and Patrick Jephson's resignation letter. It was fairly well-known that she had been to The Priory to interview George, and the Prince's Office felt that this was an act on Diana's part to discredit the Prince, while the placing of the tape in the box was no secret either.

When Diana died, Paul Burrell and others were very keen to seize this mahogany box and other artefacts. Sarah McCorquodale, who retrieved the box, is adamant that she gave a tape to Burrell – but to this day, nobody knows where this tape is.

Diana often said that she ruled by the heart not the head, but had that been the case with this matter? Perhaps it is more likely to be a combination – she was a kind woman and would no doubt have reached out to George Smith and never have automatically condemned in the way of some others, but she would also have been left with dynamite on a tape which recorded his full allegation and who knows what else.

It has been suggested that the allegation came to be reported initially by the Princess of Wales but this is categorically untrue. In the Peat Report, Sandy Henney, the Prince of Wales's press officer, graphically states: 'All we had was one poor, sad individual making an allegation of assault some years before to the Princess, who, at that time, quite frankly wanted to find ways of hurting/embarrassing her husband.' Furthermore, when household official Mrs Yaxley wrote to the Princess of Wales requesting a copy of the notes made with George Smith in the summer of 1996, Diana replied: 'I am afraid that I am unable to accede to your request because I have made a commitment of confidentiality to George.'

Published on 13 March 2003, the investigation which preceded publication looked at four main questions:

Was there an improper cover-up of the rape allegation made by George Smith in 1996?

Was there anything improper or remiss in the conduct of the Prince of Wales's household with respect to the termination of the Burrell trial?

Have official gifts given to the Prince of Wales been sold?

Have any staff in the Prince of Wales Household received improper payments or benefits?

That those questions were being asked at all was really quite remarkable. The investigation had no power to compel the cooperation of those identified and indeed both Paul Burrell and Harold Brown (Burrell's predecessor as butler) declined to be involved.

Unless and until that tape is ever recovered, we'll never have closure on this matter.

CHAPTER 12

ROS COWARD

'I have a woman's instinct and it's
always a good one.'

WHAT DID DIANA mean to people? And why are we still talking about her? On the most basic level, she seemed to embody three things – beauty, kindness and love – and it is these three elements that still draw people to her today as an icon of compassion. But the way her life so vividly and publicly also personified heartbreak and the struggle to mend her existence mean that people also relate to her as 'everywoman', a person who suffered, as most people do in their lives. Twenty-five years after her shocking death people are still debating who the real person was behind the icon, trying to understand who Diana was, and what was her significance. From my perspective, it is almost impossible to do so without looking at the late Princess of Wales through a feminist lens. For that to happen, we have to take another step backwards and look at what we mean by 'feminism' in this context. Diana was no radical feminist trailblazer; she wasn't on the balcony at Kensington Palace in suffragette colours chanting 'Down with the patriarchy!', but she did both challenge and undermine generations of royal male control with her behaviour, as well as struggling to lead a fulfilling life away from her husband.

As a mother, Diana did things her own way as far as she was able. It is impossible to overestimate the battles she faced and the barriers which were in her way, but she had an idea of the mother she wanted to be and she achieved that within extraordinary restrictions. What must be remembered is that her sons were not just *her* sons, they were ours. Royalty rules by consent and Diana was canny enough to know that she had to give her children to her adoring public in some way so that a connection developed. She was initially generous to the media with access to the children. But perhaps she was also doing that in a more calculated way, to control this access, instead of William and Harry being continually stalked by a press that felt starved. Royalists and Republicans alike shared in the births, presentations and growing of Diana's boys, and as such, in her development as a mother.

Diana's struggles resonated with many women. The woman facing her husband's affair, the woman facing unfeeling in-laws, the young mother trying to raise children in a more modern way, the woman expected to put on a show when her heart is breaking – they all saw themselves in Diana. Which is not to say that Diana could in any way appreciate the ground-down day-to-day juggling of such women. Even so there was a connection between both groups. Women saw the love she had for her children and the love she brought to her charity work; they also saw the love she wanted to pour into a marriage which was arguably disintegrating from the very start. At the time, many of them thought, *I understand that; I can see what she's going through.*

Not only did Diana's brand of mothering bring a new layer to what we had seen of past royal mothers, but it also showed us in stark relief the stereotypical and enduring masculinity of the royal men. The belief that William and Harry would follow a set path – one which had been almost carved in stone for centuries before they were born – was not one their mother would simply accept; and by deciding that she wouldn't, Diana set herself up against generations of men who 'knew best'. These were not just the men of the Royal Family, but the men in grey suits whom she often railed against, the men whose ingrained entitlement at all levels diminished and minimised what she could bring to the parenting of 'the heir and the spare'.

Charles undoubtedly felt that the parenting he had received was sub-par in a number of ways, but he also knew his place. It was not for him to have experienced what 'normal' children would have. He had a future which was pre-ordained and that future could never have included what Diana wanted for their children. There are competing views of the childhood Diana was given, but she obviously had many happy experiences and she was loved by both of her parents, even though their divorcing was painful for her. She clearly tried to reproduce the fun side of her fractured childhood. In recent years, as we have watched William and Kate forge their own path as a father and mother, the issue of different types of mothering has raised its head again. Once more, there has been scrutiny of a family trying to do things differently. When Kate Middleton first entered public consciousness most of the media barbs were levelled at her and her mother – Waity Katy and the air hostess – while the men escaped such brutal character assassinations. As time has gone on, there has been something of a change. After George and Charlotte were born, the loving, upper middle-class upbringing of Kate and her siblings was seen as a very positive, stabilising thing. Important times such as birthdays and Christmases, spent with the Middletons, were seen as Kate and William giving their children a 'normal' childhood. They would not be given their gifts on Christmas Eve, they would not be expected to sit quietly rather than enjoy rather rambunctious family gatherings – they could be young, they could be normal. After the birth of Louis a consensus seems to have emerged that the Middletons bring something immensely welcome to the Royal Family.

With Diana, the spectre of her divorced parents and the whispers about Johnny's treatment of his wife never quite settled into one accepted narrative. Family and school teachers speak of a child who was extremely naturally caring, but was sometimes insecure and unhappy about her parents' divorce. We simply don't know what the effects of her childhood were on her, whereas we can see that Kate is extremely close to her parents. Diana had to forge her own path without much significant back-up and, in doing so, brought a populist touch to royal child-rearing that had never been seen before, but which endeared her to the vast majority of the British public.

Diana's love and kindness were also very much in evidence in her interactions with the public. She much preferred those events to anything more formally imposed upon her. During her time as the Princess of Wales, the entire country was going through radical change and this coincided – or was perhaps the reason for – a vast proliferation of charities and support organisations. From domestic violence to homelessness, Diana was at the forefront of the issues that dominated and defined the 1980s and 1990s. While she worked tirelessly for them, she also gained personal recognition and a degree of independence through that work. Ironically, the lack of support from the Palace for much of what she did afforded her the chance to set her own agenda. Whether through bulimia, HIV/AIDS or landmines, we came to know the Diana she wanted to be: a modern woman with a keen commitment to socio-political issues who desperately wanted to make a difference. In the last years of her life she saw herself as a 'humanitarian', someone devoted to bettering the lot of those suffering. The way in which she put herself down as 'thick' and lacking in formal education worked in her favour – if she could do something, we all could. We didn't need a degree to see what was happening in our country, Diana was *showing* us.

Through her sons and through her work, the Princess of Wales was creating herself – and it didn't hurt matters that she did so with an image that sold millions of copies of any magazine cover she graced. Her remarkably photogenic looks were a reminder that all women can attempt to break the mould, but they have a head start if they're beautiful. From the moment she arrived on the royal 'scene' at her first official engagement, clad in a black silk ballgown, the public had a new vision of a queen-in-waiting – a beautiful, 'sexy' woman. It was a departure from everything in the past. Media coverage of the Queen had been dutiful; she had escaped constant intrusion during her youth as the Palace exercised almost complete control (as well as the limited technology of the time) and Princess Anne had never been exactly media friendly. There had been moments with Princess Margaret, but nothing would compare with this new addition to the Firm.

By the time she had done her duty of providing one son, the rumours that she was having an affair were treated rather hypocritically. There were plenty of stories about Charles being especially close to Mrs Parker Bowles – and having been so for some time – but any hint that Diana might look for comfort elsewhere was much more controversial. It took time for the public to give up the illusion that she was the perfect princess, and they found it so hard to reconcile the Diana they thought they knew with the woman revealed through Bashir and Morton. How could a perfect princess cut herself, or suffer from bulimia? How could such an icon throw herself downstairs, or endure post-natal depression? Yet the response was not one of disapproval, but of connection. The flawed but purposeful woman who gradually revealed herself was struggling with the same life issues.

The public response to Diana in both life and death reflects the complexity of the woman herself. Despite what she claimed, her instinct was not always good and that was certainly shown in her romantic life. The instinct that worked terrifically well, however, was that between her and the public, the people who saw and appreciated her love, her kindness and her beauty also appreciated that she had suffered as they had, that she had tried to turn her life around after her divorce, and that she had struggled to create meaning from her work. They also saw a woman embracing her sexuality and the power it gave her. She wasn't a feminist, but she was important for feminism.

It is no stretch to say that Diana turned the monarchy upside down, and that there are still reverberations from her behaviour and approach – she may have left us, but she has also left her mark.

CHAPTER 13

KEN WHARFE

'Everyone needs to be valued. Everyone has the potential to give something back.'

IF WE WANT to understand the story of Diana, we need to look at Paul Burrell. Ertswhile 'rock' of the Princess and stalwart of many reality shows since her death, Burrell has positioned himself as the man who knows more than many, but despite his acquittal, his reputation will always be tarnished by his trial for theft of the late Princess's possessions.

To be perfectly honest, some of those close to events never really understood why Burrell was at the Palace in the first place. What is interesting, and has never actually been said before, is how Burrell came to be the butler for the Prince and Princess of Wales. From what I understand, from Harold Brown (the long-time butler before Burrell arrived) and others who worked within the Royal Household at the time, Burrell would say that he was very fond of the Queen and that the Queen was very fond of him. So, why did he leave Buckingham Palace in the first place if he was so well-liked and adored being there? I do know that he approached Brown and requested that he ask Diana as to whether there was a space for him at Kensington Palace, but he has never been terribly forthcoming about why he did that in the first place.

Diana told me that she quite categorically said, 'No, we don't have a vacancy. Also, my husband wouldn't want it anyway.' Charles couldn't justify, in the mid-1980s, having a second butler.

In a fit of pique and panic, Brown pushed Diana on the issue and she eventually relented, saying, 'Okay, I'll speak to my husband and Burrell can go and work at Highgrove.'

Paul Burrell and his family then left Buckingham Palace and went to Highgrove. While the country environment and conditions of employment suited Burrell and his family, his obsession with the Princess was obvious and, within a very short period of time, the Prince became convinced that he was being spied on by Burrell, who was passing information on his life back to Kensington and Diana. At that point, now that he was a fully-employed butler, Burrell was sent to Kensington Palace and achieved the goal he had set out to acquire in the first place. He then began to make things rather difficult for Brown, who was a loyal, consummate butler. Brown found his position being overtaken and, in the end, left, going to work for Princess Margaret. Burrell was now very well ensconced within the Royal Household. He then, at that point, certainly in the early 1990s, raised his own status and became symptomatic of those in the Royal Household who wished to take a similar route.

Amongst other things, the Peat Report looked into the issue of gifting within the Royal Household – particularly those gifts which came back into the country after royal tours abroad, who was given these gifts, and whether people were selling them off.

The Peat Report also looked at the culture of gifting. I went to the Middle East with Diana, where wealthy Arabs would hand out watches like bags of sweets, some of them quite valuable. Nothing needed to be declared in those days. It would all come back to Kensington Palace and get divvied up within the household, or shall we say, 'redirected'. I remember coming back from Africa and someone had given the Prince of Wales an 8ft toy giraffe – what on earth would he do with that? I have no idea where that or anything else went. The internal inquiry made recommendations that from that point on, all gifts needed to be properly recorded. It was part of the Peat Report, but even if it wasn't the main issue, it does relate to the matter of Burrell.

In a recent meeting with Harold Brown, I was anxious to find out why Burrell had come to work with Diana and Charles in the first place as that has always niggled at me – and Harold Brown was the only one who could shed some light on it all. Brown is a very likeable man, who was, right up until the end of his professional career, the consummate butler. He had been a junior footman at the Palace for many, many years and in 1981 he was asked by the Queen to be the butler to Charles and Diana. By 1987/88, once Charles and Diana had separated – not officially – he was spending most of his time at Highgrove and Diana was spending most of her time in London. Occasionally they would meet for the sake of the children at Highgrove. This meant that Harold Brown was never off, he was split between two venues and, as he said to me, 'I was at breaking point. I couldn't see any way out of this, and I was told there was no budget for any additional valets.' In the end, he took it upon himself to speak to a colleague at Buckingham Palace to see if there were any suitable people available that would be an under-butler, primarily to help out at Highgrove. He didn't remember who he spoke to about that, but it would probably have been a senior steward who put forward the name of Paul Burrell.

Burrell was keen to move out because he had allegedly been involved in a controversy known as 'the Royal Yacht scandal', supposedly a homosexual orgy aboard HMY *Britannia* at a time – 1981 – when homosexuality was still illegal in the armed services. This came to the attention of the Queen, who told him, 'You have to get your life sorted out. Get married and settle down.' Surprisingly enough, he did. He married the Duke of Edinburgh's maid, and, according to Harold, saw this opportunity as a way to change his life. I'm still not sure why he left if he was such a great asset for the Queen and she was so invested in him – even after I talked to Harold Brown.

Anyway, Burrell came and went to work at Highgrove, where he was given a very nice house and he primarily looked after the Prince of Wales. Harold said, 'When he arrived here, the thing I remember about Paul Burrell was that he wanted to be a celebrity.' Harold was the exact opposite. Within a reasonable period of time, a couple of years, he was back at Kensington Palace simply because the Prince himself was unhappy with Burrell, who he sensed was spying on him, or at least passing information back. When the Prince was on his own, Camilla would be there, and Diana was now getting information back about Camilla so it had to come from one source. Burrell eventually came back to Kensington Palace and that really caused a problem as you had two butlers in a relatively small palace. There was only space for one. He was in competition with Brown.

Another matter of importance was that Brown went about his duty and wasn't fazed by celebrities, despite meeting so many, whereas Paul Burrell would ingratiate himself. According to Harold Brown, towards the end of his time there, he was actually ringing up Tom Hanks, a contact Diana had made and was very friendly with, and who wanted to help in whatever way he could with any of her charities. As Harold recalled, Burrell took it upon himself to speak to Hanks, which apparently annoyed Diana a great deal, leading her to say to the butler, 'We need to speak,' some months before she died in 1997. Brown also said that the reason Burrell was doing this with Hanks, and others, was that he was fearful that he was about to lose his job and was looking for a high-profile position with an American celebrity. Brown also said that every Tuesday, he would wind the palace clocks, about twenty or thirty of them. Paul Burrell never remembered to do this and he and Brown fell out as a result. In the end, Diana said to Brown – this would have been in 1995 – 'Why are you spying on me?'

Harold was shocked. 'I've never spied on anybody. Why would I spy on you, Ma'am? This is my life, I've been in royal service my entire life. Who said I was spying?'

Diana told the Queen this and the Queen told Princess Margaret. Princess Margaret's butler, a man called John Leishman, had died not long before, and Harold saw an exit as he felt his move was to some extent being planned. In a discussion with her about what Diana had said, Princess Margaret forcefully said, 'You're going nowhere, Harold, you're staying here.' Harold then transferred and spent the next seven years working for Princess Margaret, saying it was one of his most defining moments as a royal butler. That question from Diana in 1995 about 'Why are you spying on me?' all fits in with what happened to me in 1993/94 and the paranoia she was displaying, coupled with what happened with the

Martin Bashir interview. The one thing, according to her brother, which cemented the interview was that Bashir said he had evidence that people very close to Diana were actually spying on her and were in conversations with MI5, myself included.

Meeting and talking with Harold Brown in 2022 confirmed to me how Burrell came to be at Kensington Palace and the mayhem which ensued after his arrival. We have now seen that he seems to be obsessed with celebrity and seems to take part in everything he is offered.

Harold said, 'Paul was fearful of being sacked and would cry with me repeatedly. I regretted enormously supporting the position of him. I had no choice, I was overworked with two houses to keep, but I just wish Paul had never brought that wish for celebrity with him. When he was here, it was very difficult for me to get rid of him.'

There were numerous celebrities who came to Kensington Palace in the 1990s – Elton John, George Michael, many film stars who were all part of the Diana charity base – and they all wanted a piece of this action for their own good cause or charity. Whereas Harold would deal with it in a very professional way, Paul would ingratiate himself in their company and clearly had a diary with the telephone numbers of these people. Even Burrell himself has written that he was looking for another position in America with somebody – anybody – of celebrity status. This was typical of the Paul Burrell I knew.

Early one morning we came back from a gym session because Diana wasn't feeling particularly well. As we arrived, she went upstairs and I went into the butler's pantry, where I could always learn what was going on. Paul was there but left when I arrived. I heard Diana laughing quite soon after that and also the sound of Paul whining. I went out of the butler's pantry and there was the stairwell that led up into the apartment. Paul Burrell was caressing Diana's shoeless feet.

'What the hell's going on?' I asked. 'Ma'am? What's up?'

'I've just found *him* going through my desk,' she replied.

'What?'

'It's true. He was going through my desk.'

'Is that right, Paul?' I demanded.

'Oh no, no, no ...' he whimpered.

'Just get up, will you? Just get up!'

He did so, and I was clear with Diana about Burrell. 'Ma'am, under such circumstances you have to speak with Patrick – you've got to get rid of him.' It was the only reaction I could have. He went crying off somewhere and that was it. It was really bizarre.

Burrell was an extraordinary character. In my view this idea of him being Diana's rock was a figment of his imagination. I remember Frances Shand Kydd saying to me, 'I don't know where he got this bloody rock business from. As far as I'm concerned, you all were.' The problem with Paul was that he had this innate jealousy that he always wanted to be with 'his' Princess. Once she left the Palace, he was bereft but he simply couldn't follow her everywhere. It wasn't his role. The powerful thing for him and anybody in service like this is that they always have their Princess, or whoever, last thing at night and first thing in the morning. Dealing with her absence and another member of the household being with her during the day was a problem for Burrell. Harold Brown didn't mind, most professional butlers wouldn't, but Burrell did.

When Diana died, there was an extraordinary state of affairs which concluded in Paul Burrell being charged with theft. He was accused of stealing hundreds, if not thousands, of Diana's possessions – including the mahogany box which allegedly contained the interviews Diana had conducted in The Priory with George Smith.

The Peat Report stated that Burrell had been entrusted with that tape after Diana's death by her sister, Lady Sarah McCorquodale. I wasn't privy to any of the George Smith case but I knew him well – personally, I feel he was not someone who would tell a lie. He didn't know how to deal with things – he didn't want to lose his position, so he found himself in a huge dilemma. He told the Private Secretary about the rape but no one believed him. A judgment was made and they decided it could never have happened, and that Smith had a drinking problem which necessitated his stay in The Priory, paid for by the Prince. If Burrell did have that tape, and if it was made public, who knows what it would have done to the Royal Family?

In the Peat Report, it's asked, 'Who was given the tape?' Sarah McCorquodale, Diana's sister, said, 'I gave it to Burrell for safe-keeping as I had a dental appointment.' He denied ever having it.

We now know that when Diana died, Paul Burrell took hundreds of items, letters, dresses, personal items, and stored them in the roof of his house, and the roof of his mother's next door. The decision was taken as to whether Burrell should be investigated, along with Harold Brown. In the end, the police were involved and both men were arrested on the suspicion of theft of Diana's property. The charges against Brown were dropped almost immediately. In complete contrast, Burrell was eventually charged with numerous counts of theft of Diana's property. If someone breaks into your house and steals a few dresses, a few books, a few letters, you'd be lucky if you got the cleaner from the local police station to come out and see you. In this case, because of the high nature of the complainant, in other words, the Royal Family, Scotland Yard put at their disposal detectives from the Serious Crime Squad to investigate the allegation of theft.

The prospect of a trial of the man who had seen so much, was privy to so much, was an extraordinary matter. This inquiry was headed up by the Serious Crime Squad at Scotland Yard, headed by a man called John Yates. Detective Inspector Maxine de Brunner headed an investigation team under the direction of Commander Yates. These were experienced detectives effectively looking into an allegation of substantial theft. De Brunner and her team were having trouble sifting through the below-stairs menagerie of staff and wanted to know the system. They wouldn't know what an under-butler was, nor a Lady of the Bedchamber. At the time, although I wasn't working for Diana, I recall my boss, Commander Peter Clarke, calling me in.

'Look, we need your help, Ken.'

'Really?'

'You know we're investigating the Burrell thing?'

'I've heard about that.'

'Well, the detectives on it are finding it difficult to find their way through this rabbit run of below-stairs activity. You know the set-up there probably better than anyone. Can you help with this?'

'Okay – what's in it for me? What do I get out of this?' I didn't mean that in the sense of a pecuniary advantage, I could just see this going wrong and I needed to know where it would leave me. I agreed to see de Brunner and the others for about a week or so, telling them as much as I knew. During those meetings, they raised the subject of Burrell and this tape, when the name of George Smith came up. I tried to explain it all in simple terms, allowing them to carry on with the investigation.

'Did you know George Smith?'

'Yes, I knew him very well.'

'What's your take on this?'

'What's my take? Well, let's put it this way – George Smith was a recommendation from his colonel-in-chief in the Welsh Guards, he was a veteran from the Falklands War, he jumped ship off the burning *Sir Galahad*; the guy was trustworthy. He wouldn't have been recommended to work for the Prince of Wales had he not been so. I found him to be someone who found transferring from Army life to the Palace a bit of a shock, he was decked out in a way that was in complete contrast to his previous life. But he was an honest and loyal servant. I knew him very well.'

The next thing, I got a phone call from Peter Clarke's deputy saying they had been informed: 'Tell Wharfe to back off. We don't need him anymore.'

'Ah,' I thought, 'this is all because I started mentioning George Smith, even though it was in response to a question.'

That was the last involvement I had with it all.

I have only recently discovered that the initial route for the information to be brought to the attention of the police was through Harold Brown. Burrell was involved as the jewel-encrusted Arab dhow which it was alleged Brown had stolen was up for sale at Spinks, the auction house. Brown then said to the police, 'Hang on, there are other people involved in this.' Brown's case was dismissed but once the investigation got underway, thousands of items of property were discovered in Burrell's home. He had so much stuff that it was like walking into a room at Buckingham Palace. Burrell wanted the recent pictures of Diana and her children. It was almost a shrine to them. He tried to write to William and Harry during this period to say that he'd only done it for them. He was denied access and I have no idea if they ever received that letter. It would have been possible to look at CCTV to see how he managed to get everything out – there was even a desk that had been taken, which could not exactly have been smuggled out in his pockets. As far as I am aware, that was never done.

Burrell went for trial and was charged with multiple cases of theft, 301 items actually, worth over four million pounds. The Crown Prosecution Service agreed that there was a case to answer; because of the public interest in the case, and due to the high profile of the matter, instead of going to the local magistrates' court, it went to the Old Bailey. Burrell was represented by Lord Carlile, an eminent criminal barrister, and it was the showcase of the world. From my policing experience, very few people go to the Old Bailey if there is lack of evidence. The case was presented by a team of experienced detectives from the Serious Crime Squad, investigating a burglary, really – someone breaking into someone's house and stealing their property. Not so difficult, you would have thought, as the evidence was pretty easy to gather. Both de Brunner and her team would have recommended this case to the CPS, who would have only recommended taking it forward if they thought there was a realistic chance of prosecution. The case went for trial.

On day eleven of the trial, the Crown Prosecutor was told by Commander John Yates of Scotland Yard that he had just spoken with Peat and there had been a remarkable recollection. A few days earlier, the Duke of Edinburgh and the Prince of Wales were in a car going towards the City to another engagement. Suddenly, the Queen remembered that she had given him authority to remove these items of property and informed her husband, the Duke of Edinburgh. The case was conveniently stopped. If she knew, then it couldn't have been theft after all.

End of story.

Burrell was acquitted and said, 'The Queen came through for me.' We have to ask, why did he feel that way? Let us reflect upon that just a little more. Burrell was accused of stealing Diana's property. It went as far as the Old Bailey, which was no small matter. Eventually, the Queen conveniently recalled, *Oh yes – I remember now, I told him he could do that.*

When I left in 2002, I was very keen to find out what had happened. I had no other motive, apart from being intrigued. In my opinion, the Queen should have been asked at the very beginning if she had given authority or allowed someone else to do so. Somehow that had not happened. I spoke to Maxine de Brunner, by now a senior police officer in the Metropolitan Police, having never met her before.

'Would it be possible to meet?' I had asked her.

'Why?'

'I'd like to discuss the Burrell case if possible – I'd be keen to know why you thought the case collapsed, given your expertise and the system.'

'There's no point, Ken.'

'Why is that?'

'Well, you know what happened, I know what happened and I can't say any more than that.'

Now, Burrell is quite important, after my involvement in Diana's life as he had made himself out to be completely indispensable to her. There is no way that the Royals could ever have allowed that trial to fully go ahead and allow him to no doubt make huge revelations, but the fact that it went so far, that it went to the wire, was extraordinary. You have to ask why someone didn't ask the Queen beforehand if she gave Burrell that permission. One of her many courtiers could have sorted that out in an instant. I'm sceptical of the assertion that she was not asked – it was a theft case, simple as that, but I couldn't possibly say why she had that sudden flash of memory so long afterwards. The level of expertise in the Serious Crime Squad would surely have asked probing questions very early on and one would expect her memory to have been jogged at that point. No one is above the law, not even the Queen, but there would have been a series of protocols to adhere to in such a serious case. There was a great deal of public interest – the trial had begun, and if the Queen hadn't remembered, this would all have gone much further. The fact of the matter is, one of the ways to stop it was for the Queen to say what she did.

The police found many things in Burrell's loft, but they didn't check the loft next door. Interestingly, Burrell had a house in America, he sold many stories and was reimbursed financially. He had letters from William, photographs, and more – I can only assume the property that was seized was returned to its rightful owners in due course.

How he came to have all these items remains a matter for conjecture. However good his relations with the Queen might have been, it seems most unlikely that she would have allowed him to take into his custody the personal effects of a senior member of the

Royal Family who had just died. So there was surely a case against Burrell . . . except that any trial would have ultimately revealed the existence of the mahogany box, and would then have exposed what was on the tape inside it – which may have been a powder keg for the Royal Household.

Harold Brown said to me, 'Burrell had an extraordinary life,' which is true, but there are a great many questions hanging over much of that life. Burrell was reportedly involved in the Royal Yacht scandal in 1981 when he claimed there had been a gay orgy onboard the *Britannia*. The Queen was kept up to date on proceedings into the case – homosexuality was still illegal in the British military at that time, hence the disciplinary investigation and subsequent dismissals – and she is considered to be fairly broad-minded. It is believed that was the point where she encouraged Burrell to settle down, or he would have to find another position – and two years later, he married his wife, Maria, and was reinstated within the Queen's household.

Burrell was the prancing leopard who couldn't change his spots; he had any number of gay affairs after the yacht scandal and while at Kensington Palace. He was a bit of a liability. Diana liked him as he was a gossip. He was a means to an end really. Diana asked Harold at one point, 'Why are you spying on me?' but in my view the best spy she ever had was Paul Burrell. That was the reason he left Highgrove – because Charles was suspicious, thinking that Burrell was spying on him for Diana. Burrell felt he was important, the link telling her what was going on with Charles, and he made life systematically very difficult for many people in the Palace.

I do feel that there are still some unanswered questions on this matter. Many will be unhappy that this will be raised again, they'll say the Queen is ninety-six and it's unfair, but, for me, this is extremely relevant to Diana's life, and it was a big issue in her life. The whole paranoia set in, the fear that Martin Bashir encouraged – she was terrified of people turning against her and this began as early as 1993 when I was there. There is no evidence to suggest she spoke to Bashir before that and he's never said anything, I think it's unlikely he ever will, but to what extent was Burrell fanning the flames?

Diana grew in confidence after the Morton book – if she'd lost friends in the royal circle, that didn't bother her as they were gone anyway, she didn't have any real friends there. She did say to me that she was close to Princess Margaret, but I couldn't honestly confirm if that was the case; there was certainly nobody else there who was a confidante. The late Duke of Edinburgh was sympathetic and understanding, and she told me on numerous occasions the nice things that he had said in letters, but apart from that the circle was closed against her. Her sisters found the situation difficult, but their loyalty stood firm and stayed with her – I saw no family breakdown although her mother probably spat blood for a while. I've never known her brother to talk publicly about it but in my personal discussions with him, I do feel that he too thought it was the only way for Diana to get her side of things out there.

Of course, Spencer was highly involved in the Bashir interview when the latter presented him with a bag of lies, a dossier of fake news in an attempt to convince him and his sister that everyone was against her. Once that got back to Diana, it would have dropped very neatly into her box and she would have said, 'That's what I'm talking about, this doesn't surprise me.' That dossier did convince her that there was every reason to give the interview to the BBC. It has to be said that Charles Spencer was suspicious of Bashir, and rightly so as we now know the thirty-five 'facts' were largely lies. The Dyson Inquiry in 2020–1 found Bashir to be wanting and the matter is still ongoing – her Private Secretary, Patrick Jephson, had to resign as his position was no longer tenable after it all came to light. He had not been informed or consulted by Diana ahead of the Bashir interview, and felt that as her private secretary he should have been. Given that he had no idea what was going on, he could hardly remain in place.

I don't think Diana manipulated either Morton or Bashir, I think she was simply desperate to get the facts across. The story was growing and growing, and the decision had to come from her as the other side was too powerful. Nicholas Soames, after all, went on *Newsnight* and said she was 'paranoid'. Lady Kennard, a friend of the Queen, described Diana as 'damaged goods'. In my time with her, I witnessed that Diana was in very good health – there was no sign of bulimia at that time – and very focused on her role. But she was stuck on how to resolve things and her decision to open up made her seem a loose cannon.

Every single day that she stepped out of the gates at Kensington Palace, there was either someone lurking at the bottom of the drive or wherever we ended up, where there would be a mass turnout of media. They weren't just there to cover the story, but were present in anticipation that something else might come out. That's how explosive this bomb was – it was building, everyone knew something would happen at some point as little bits were floating out all the time that there was something wrong with Diana's marriage. The late James Whitaker from the *Daily Mirror* was very wise and knew they couldn't afford to miss a trick; he knew she had to be followed across the world on bottomless expenses from Fleet Street. When Kate and William travel, you'll now be lucky to get five or six journalists with them – there's no gossip there, there's nothing to justify the media following them. But with Diana, it was uncontrollable. As long as Diana was there, the story was there.

The Royal Family didn't really look at changes in society or culture or media. Instead they blamed it all on Diana. They wanted nothing more than for her to fade into oblivion but if they had approached this in a different way, it could have all been so different. She always said, 'I'm the problem.' And she was. Every single day, the Royal Family story was about her, not anyone else. Most of it was good, but she was the key to it all and they didn't like being knocked off the top perch. If you think of it another way, a senior executive going into a company, who brings attention, increased awareness, adulation and a higher profile will be told what a great job they're doing – Diana achieved all of that for the Firm, and they gave her little in return. The Queen or Princess Anne would simply put out their gloved hand and say, 'How are you?' or 'Have you come far?' Diana would take her gloves off, crouch down beside children, engage everyone and make them feel special. That was what no one else could bring themselves to do. For all the Prince's commendable charitable causes, he has very little in the way of a 'human' approach. If Charles and Diana were together, it was striking – he would glance behind him as Diana lingered with people; he clearly couldn't understand how she worked or why she was more popular. The answer was clear – it was simply who she was.

In terms of whether Diana *did* manipulate the media, one of the oft-mentioned 'examples' are the images of her sitting alone in front of the Taj Mahal, poignant in her solitude. I was there for those Taj Mahal photos, one of the last joint tours they did. The Prince always knew that scene at the Temple of Love would be a problem. The last thing he wanted was to be seen sat with his wife there when we all knew what was going on. Conveniently, he went off to another engagement and left Diana to do the visit alone – the headlines were pretty much printed before she left the Indian High Commission as far as I was concerned. We arrived there with a massive media entourage, and I think only two went with the Prince. The image of that trip was Diana alone in front of the Taj Mahal – she didn't manipulate that, the press location had already been set up, and I suspect the same bench is used for every important visitor. She looked at it and said to me out of the corner of her mouth, 'What am I going to do?'

'You're going to have to sit there, whether you like it or not,' I told her. So she did and, of course, there was a massive cacophony of camera noises. It was Simon McCoy of Sky News at that time who shouted out, 'What does it feel like, Your Royal Highness?'

Under her breath, she said to me, 'What a stupid question! What shall I say?'

'I don't know – I'm no scriptwriter!' Royal correspondent, Dickie Arbiter should have been doing all that, but I have no idea where he was. 'Just say it's a healing experience or something like that.'

She went with that but a journalist at the front said, 'What do you mean by that?'

Quick as ever, Diana responded, 'Work it out for yourself.' That brought quite a chuckle of laughter. She got up and whispered to me, 'God, I think that was the worst thing I've done in my life!'

We moved on, the Taj Mahal dealt with. You can see why the Prince wouldn't have wanted to be involved with that situation; his presence would have brought extraordinary coverage and a picture of them both there together would have caused an even bigger furore.

I was asked at the marriage of Harry and Meghan about the similarities with the bride and Princess Diana. They are obviously both attractive and incredibly popular – but the almost instant popularity got the better of Meghan. During their extraordinary wedding at Windsor – which was a great day – you could see the bewilderment on the faces of the Royal Family. What was going on? Why was no one sticking to tradition? Who was this mad minister and why was there a gospel choir? In any normal wedding, everyone stays together afterwards and has a party, they did of sorts following a horse drawn carriage ride through Windsor but for this young couple, they were on their own, off to Frogmore Cottage, an isolated dwelling in the grounds of Windsor Castle – and a gift from Her Majesty. I don't think Meghan expected any of this and it must have been a very difficult lifestyle for both of them in the subsequent months. Perhaps she thought that she would immediately be put into high-profile, somewhat glamorous positions, but even Diana didn't have that immediately – she had to work for what she got, and she got little acclaim from the Royals for doing so.

I wasn't surprised that they went to live in Canada, then California. Harry said, 'I don't want Meghan to suffer the way my mother suffered,' but I think he would be very unlikely to remember the early years with Diana. If you look at the lack of interaction between the rest of the Royal Family and Meghan, it certainly doesn't look as though Harry and Meghan perceived it as being very friendly, and I imagine that Meghan would have found it difficult in the same way that Diana did. I doubt it was what she had expected in any way. We are now hearing gossip that she didn't enjoy her first tour in Australia, and that she allegedly found it a 'waste of time' – no one can know such things for sure (other than her husband, I suppose), but the fact that Meghan has been turned into someone in the public mind who *would* say things like that is highly indicative of how relatively fickle the support for the young couple seems to have been.

Diana was neither manipulator or manipulated – it was just the way things were. Every time we went out of the gates, there was a photographer, who knew the law, and knew they had every right to be there. Getting angry with them would have achieved nothing – I just had to find a diplomatic way of dealing with it and work out the best thing for Diana. I think she dealt with it all very well and gave a good performance in the theatre that is the Royal Family, as part of the Monarchy Show. Will anyone else ever be likely to be able to replicate that? I doubt it, but only time will tell.

CHAPTER 14

ROS COWARD

"I want to walk into a room, be it a hospital for the dying or a hospital for the sick children and feel that I am needed, I want to do, not just to be.'

Once Diana was 'out' of the Firm, she was at risk, not because she was taking risks but because, after it was clear that the marriage had fallen apart, that it wasn't salvageable, and they were on the pathway from separation to divorce, she tried to lead a normal life in abnormal circumstances. She was especially concerned to give the children some kind of normality but, particularly after the divorce when Royal protection had been withdrawn, this was difficult and potentially risky. It was Diana herself who refused protection, but it is puzzling why the Queen didn't insist on it, because there were many shocking incidents that happened towards the end of Diana's life when the press completely swarmed around her. In the interview with Martin Bashir she described how the early agreeable relationship she had had with the press had broken down, with the paparazzi openly harassing her and the children. It is possible, likely, even, that she would have accepted protection if the Queen had made that call.

Post-divorce, Diana didn't have the kind of protection she should have had, and this was almost certainly a contributing factor in her death. Had she had a security person such as Ken, whose first and foremost aim would be to protect her, he would have been looking out for what could have been done differently on that last evening in 1997. As it was, the security they had was Dodi's, answering to the Fayeds, and there was certainly a potential conflict of interest there. I'm not suggesting any sort of conspiracy theory, far from it, but there are unanswered questions about why Diana was so poorly protected, why no one in the car insisted on her wearing a seat belt. Maybe Diana could have changed things. She would probably have known the people protecting her lacked the expertise. She did, as she'd worked with security before, she knew what should happen so why didn't she say something? She could have done, but perhaps it was all dependent on the impact that Dodi Fayed had on her in those days they were together.

Diana really was trying to lead some semblance of a normal life, and inevitably this led her into wanting to do things that a lot of the Royals simply wouldn't have done. Although there may be an unwritten understanding when someone marries into the Royal Family, it's not one that they're very good at revealing to the other side. This was a perennial theme in Diana's life – there were expectations, but nobody ever shared them with her or gave her guidance about what they were. She was just thrown in at the deep end and expected to know everything. In that period after her engagement, when she was waiting to be married and was a bit hidden away, many accounts confirm that there was no advice at all. When she expressed some doubts about the forthcoming marriage, her sister said, 'Too late now – you're on all the tea towels.' That was about it. There was never any attempt to warn her about the difficulties that lay ahead; indeed, it sounds as if she was quite seriously left on her own and had to make her own way.

Immediately after her wedding to Prince Charles, when she began to go on public walkabouts with her husband, little guidance appears to have been given. There has been a repetition with Meghan, who also appears not to have been given adequate guidance. If, for example, the Palace had intervened early on and mediated between Meghan's father and her about the wedding, some of the alienation and discord that developed between them, exploited by the British press, could perhaps have been avoided. Meghan has indicated that she wasn't given any direction or support about what was expected of her – this was clear in the Oprah Winfrey interview. It really is quite remarkable that now, after so much has been written about Diana and how much she was on her own, the Royal Family appears to still be operating the same way thirty years later.

It's an easier ride for the incomers who are more conformist, like Kate Middleton. Meghan by contrast had a career as an actress. She was an established 'grown-up', with a grown-up life. Before she met Harry she was involved in campaigning and charitable work often connected with women's causes. As a result, she has been more openly critical of her reception from the start: she could see the flaws, and was an independent person before she met Harry. Diana lived through that process in the public eye: all of her growing up, her struggle to become an independent person with a purpose, was done in public.

Much of Diana's development and learning process came from her involvement with favoured charities. She wanted to feel she was doing something meaningful and even when she withdrew from some of the charities, she was still focused on how she could be useful. In her own words, she wanted to 'do', not just 'be'. She understood the power of her own brand, and at times she used it for her purposes, even having discussions with John Major and Tony Blair about becoming a UK ambassador after her divorce – in the event, they seemed to make some promises in that direction that were never followed through.

Diana was a woman struggling with this concept of independence. It might not be our current concept of female independence, which would involve having a career and parity with men, but the journey she went on, from an inexperienced, dependent, badly treated young wife, to a powerful independent woman trying to use her position to be useful, very much chimed with themes of women's self-discovery at the time. Again, it is interesting to make a comparison with Kate Middleton. She has found a place where she is quite happy. She's never worked, she's obviously doing a lot for charity, but it's not about 'How can I be an independent woman in my own right?', whereas both Diana and Meghan grappled with that issue.

Diana's journey was also about doing family life differently, in a less traditional and repressed way. In a collection of essays about her, the historian Simon Schama spoke of her as an icon, and made the point that in 1981, when she married Charles and went on to have her first baby, we were in the throes of Thatcherite Britain. The glory days of The Beatles and Carnaby Street were over and there had, to some extent, been a swing back to this rather stern attitude of 'Nanny knows best' that Thatcher represented, of a state repression of feelings which trickled down – although whether it actually did is debatable. Diana has to be seen in that context as this young mother who actually represented what a very significant chunk of the population was thinking and feeling, set against the formal, restrictive British repression. That is an important element about her views on mothering, in particular. She may not have used the word 'repression', but so much *was* about the repression of affection and treating children with coldness. She always had a very simplistic but effective line: *There's nothing much wrong with tender, loving care.*

I remember attending a conference where she talked about how 'everyone needs a hug', and the effect was electric. It may not have been a sophisticated philosophy, but it was from the heart, all about showing love, warmth and affection. It was something she lived by. She touched her kids, she hugged them, all of the photographers remarked on how she never took her eyes off them – and this was new for the Royals. There are many iconic photographs of her with her arms out and the boys rushing into them, a very different image from the repressed, somewhat chilly, images normally associated with the Royal Family.

It was also significant that she often took her children with her on charity visits. William has recently said he intends to take George to visit homeless charities as his mother did with him. It was an acknowledgement of the significant impact these visits had on William but also a recognition that what his mother did was a considerable break from anything the Royal Family had done before. Diana very much believed that her boys should not live in a gilded cage, and they should see the sort of things she saw at, for example, the homeless charity Centrepoint. She kept in touch with people, writing to them, giving them her personal phone number, inviting them to come to tea. It was all about breaking down barriers, and the Royals had never seen anyone do that before.

A paraplegic man named Simon Barnes recalls going to one such tea at Kensington Palace. Harry was very much involved, sitting on Simon's lap while Simon did wheelies, and, by all accounts the meeting – like many others – was perfectly relaxed and informal. Diana certainly wanted her children to be involved in as much as possible and to understand that there was another side to life. Her emotional modernity and authenticity remain the breakthrough in relation to the Royal Family. Meghan might have had had a similar effect, but given that she is now ostracised with Harry in California it seems that we'll never find out. Would she have continued along the same lines as her late mother-in-law, could she have built on the popularity she initially had, or would the comparisons have been too much?

Diana was prescient in her beliefs about the need for the Royal Family to modernise, something which William has also said he wants to address. Diana's approach went deeper than bringing the children up differently; it was more along the lines of believing that the monarchy really needs to consist of people who are in touch with the country over which they reign. Diana probably understood the precariousness of the monarchy more than they did because she came to it, not just with a modernity they lacked, but with an emotional intelligence that wasn't even in their playbook. She was not well educated, but she understood that there was something to be dealt with there. She had gut responses which were extremely valid, she was quick to grasp things, but she was also professional and canny: through her charity work, she participated in some government advisory groups, and everyone was struck by how well she had managed to absorb the brief, the questions she asked and the follow-up probing she would do if the answers weren't good enough.

There is an anecdote in my book concerning a visit by Diana to one of the charities around Valentine's Day time, when she met a young lad who was actually dying. The executive of the charity was struck by her interaction with this boy when she didn't ask, 'How many Valentine's cards did you get?' but 'How many have you sent this year?' The executive said that most people would have either been crippled by embarrassment to ask that of someone who was dying, or they would have asked how many the boy had received. The fact that she asked how many he had sent showed a sensitivity and emotional quickness that she constantly demonstrated and which connected her to the public.

Diana was also incredibly witty and quick with her responses. All these elements add up to a picture of a woman who really must have hit the Royals like a bolt of lightning. They didn't get a perpetual nineteen-year-old, they didn't get someone whom they could mould because she'd been brought into the fray at such an early age – they got a force of nature. When someone like that comes along and raises questions about your very existence as royalty, about the very nature of your engagement with your people, then is it any wonder they were staggered?

Diana also fought to have her views heard. We now know that she was heavily manipulated by Martin Bashir to gain an interview and her anxieties were inflamed and made considerably worse. But in spite of this, as she showed with her secret collaboration with Andrew Morton, she managed to speak directly to the public. She ensured that her voice was heard. The day after the Bashir interview, the press were taken aback by the largely positive reaction of viewers to what Diana had said. The public heard for the first time in her own words how she had suffered, how she was trying to live her life, and her views on the monarchy.

What Diana said about Charles was very revealing about so many aspects of her concerns. She said that he didn't really want the job, that he would rather be in his country house with his 'lady'. She was hinting at what she believed the monarchy needed: not a country squire but someone who understood ordinary people and connected with them. Charles had a very different consciousness, suspicious of his wife's popularity and instinctive touch. Diana seemed to be saying in the Bashir interview that William would be better suited to the throne than his father. Certainly if William knows that things need to change in the way that Diana wished, and engages in some modernisation, that will be a fascinating experiment. But when that might be remains to be seen, and the country could be in for rather a long wait.

In terms of how these attributes contributed to Diana's legacy, we only have to look at the issues she got involved with, for she did change the public perception of them. Her sheer willingness to break taboos was shocking at the time, but she was breaking new ground. The journalists of the time, while largely liberal themselves, had no idea, for example, that she was actually going to touch someone who was HIV-positive. This was at a time of extreme fear of the illness when some people still imagined it could be spread by just touching someone. As a result gay men with

AIDS suffered terribly from being socially shunned. Those pictures went round the world, and even today there are many people who still feel strongly that what she did was bold and courageous. It is impossible to underestimate just how powerful her actions were.

Where did she find such courage and readiness to break taboos? Her mother said that 'the whole handshake issue' was quite 'self-conscious' on Diana's part. She had discussed becoming involved with AIDS charities with Frances Shand Kydd, and was quite conscious of what she was doing even though there was resistance from the Royal Family. Similarly, leprosy, mental-health issues, landmines, and charities specifically aimed at terminal illness and dying – all of those were causes you don't particularly see the Royals involving themselves with; they tend to stick to safer topics.

Diana's impact in these areas was nothing other than astonishing. In spite of her weaknesses and contradictions, her occasional attempts to gain the upper hand with Charles, in spite of her occasional mistakes in decisions like collaborating with someone like Bashir, she was more sinned against than sinning.

CHAPTER 15

KEN WHARFE

*'I just want someone to be there for me,
to make me feel safe.'*

THE COMPARISONS WITH Kate and Meghan won't
go away – the media will always make fashion comparisons
no matter how tenuous, but, more interestingly and on a deeper
level, the relationships are so opposed in terms of what Diana
experienced. Harry's mother had no option other than to support
herself in the end – that is something Meghan had pretty much
always done before she met her royal husband. Kate, on the other
hand, is very much a supporter of her husband and people tend
to look at how 'classy' she is not to push herself as bigger than the
monarchy or her husband. Really, there is very little comparison
between them despite the media trying to fabricate and generate as
much as possible.

I'm not entirely sure there are contested memories when we look
back on Diana, although that is often a topic which is discussed.
She was the victim of many things, of that there is no doubt –

towards the end of her life, yes, she did speak with journalists but I don't think it shaped her life, nor was she in regular contact with the media. It was post-Morton, I would say, when things changed. The publication of his book altered so much dramatically, that her relationship with the Royal Family at that point would never have recovered. She stayed with Charles another year after publication but knew it was over. Up until that point, any contention was over the Camilla issue, but Diana was the victim of that. She couldn't find a way through it, she couldn't find a way to resolve it and she had no one to speak to about it. Friends were very reluctant to tell her things that were likely to be controversial for fear of being excluded and this is something I witnessed quite a few times. They were happy to be with her for obvious reasons, but if there was a risk of losing that friendship – which happened with Catherine Soames, for example, who saw their friendship wane following advice that was not well received – there were problems.

I think, to be honest, she was more a victim of circumstances, up until the point of the Morton book and beyond. Post-1993/94, you could argue Diana was no longer an operational member of the Royal Family, and so became a bit of a free agent, which annoyed the Royals, and led to the Queen, with Charles, being so insistent that the divorce be brought along as quickly as possible, I suspect, to not damage the reputation of the Royal Family any further. They did see her as a damaging property and her media relationship was undoubtedly problematical. That was the only way she could spread her views to the public and they couldn't quite deal with that.

It's hard to see what Diana's alternatives could have been – how else could she play her life out while still having some control?

She had very few choices. Charles had categorically denied the relationship with Camilla until the Jonathan Dimbleby TV interview, at a point when he felt his marriage had irretrievably broken down. I had witnessed their meetings many times and knew that Diana had been right all along. She was a different character after the Morton book when divorce was inevitable. There was also a new career on offer, although she didn't quite know what that would be. A new Diana would emerge, a very different one from the one I first met.

I think that there is perhaps a contested view of Diana's childhood – I can only relate that to what Diana said to me, and the joint conversations on holiday with her sisters, or when I spent time with her and her mother in Scotland. We know the circumstances of the divorce and that her father took custody of the children – which was a landmark case really, as it was so unusual for the father to do so. Diana was the second-youngest and never said to me that it was a horrendous time, despite many people labouring that point somewhat and seeing it as a huge factor in her own pattern of mothering and being a wife. She remembered the publicity surrounding the divorce which made things rather difficult at school, but speaking to her and her siblings, it always seemed to me that it wasn't as bad as the media at the time made out. Of course, it was a good story for them that the lady of the house of a high-profile aristocratic family left her children for a sheep farmer in Australia – it's a great line – but did they have a bad childhood because of it? I don't think so.

Their aristocratic lifestyle meant they were living in a big house in the countryside, all of them privately educated. I remember going to her school with her in 1987, to West Heath in Kent, two days after the Great Storm. On that helicopter flight down there, as we witnessed the extraordinary tree damage from the air, she recalled the fun times she'd had at West Heath.

'I wasn't the brightest,' she remembered. 'I was hopeless, Ken! I wish that hadn't been the case, but I just couldn't do any of it.'

The headmistress at the time has said that too. Diana gave a speech while she was there and told them all that she'd had good times even if she hadn't excelled academically, to put it mildly. At our meeting afterwards, Miss Rudd said, 'You might not have been brightest, but you did always look as if you were enjoying yourself!' We visited Diana's dormitory and found a carving – she had etched her initials into the panelling on a wall. She reflected on the happy moments at the school. She didn't need a university education. She was a nursery teacher in Kensington when she left school, which was probably a perfectly happy position for her. Did she need to work? Probably not – she would have had financial stability anyway, and her relationship with her father was a good one so he wasn't going to cut her off or cast her out. Whenever we met him, there were always loving exchanges and she talked favourably of him. We went to Althorp a number of times, but his relationship with Raine Spencer was something that didn't sit well with Diana at that time. She hated that she was changing the whole structure of Althorp and the four siblings agreed on that. It all changed following her father's death and when Diana moved away from the clutches of royalty. Raine Spencer was actually very close to Mohamed Al-Fayed, which fits in with Diana's relationship with Dodi.

Diana's relationship with her mother, during the 1980s and up until I left, was a close one – and I would count Frances as Diana's best friend. There's never a better friend to have than your mother.

Frances was quite surprised when Diana decided to say goodbye to me in 1993 and then when she abandoned her security detail. She couldn't work out quite what her daughter was doing. Frances was quite a religious person and was unhappy about Diana's relationship with the surgeon Hasnat Khan as he was a Muslim. That shouldn't have made any difference, but it did to Frances. It's very sad that in the early to mid-1990s, Diana's relationship with her mother faded. Frances became ill and turned into quite a heavy drinker, actually being arrested for a drink-driving offence in Scotland, which didn't go down well with Diana at all. I fear she may have become a rather sad character towards the end.

In 2020, Diana's brother Charles Spencer published his dossier in which Martin Bashir's claims which secured the *Panorama* interview were laid bare. Among other claims, it suggested that I was spying on her, which was a complete fabrication. Bashir claimed he had statements that showed money had changed hands with security personnel. It was all lies. Andrew Morton told me that everybody knew this in 2004. Information had been passed to Bashir about the fact that Patrick Jephson had been taking flying lessons – this was true, but how would anybody know unless they had access to his diary? What Patrick says is that Diana wouldn't, but someone in the office must have done for this information to be passed to Bashir. In my view – and I've suggested this to Morton – it could have been one of two people. The point is, the Bashir interview destabilised Diana in the 1990s, to guarantee and secure an interview – he was successful in this. On top of the paranoia she was already experiencing, to be told that people within her close circle were actually spying on her and bank statements had been drawn up to prove that money had been paid into a fictitious account was probably enough for her to believe, *Well, actually, this could be right* – which goes right back to the year that I left, 1993. How much information was being peddled towards her about members of staff who were allegedly being disloyal, we'll never know. It's possible that process had already begun. Since Bashir has stayed quiet, one can only surmise certain things. What I do know is, in the dossier he revealed to Charles Spencer, the allegations against me are demonstrably false – I certainly never worked for Richard Aylard, nor was I ever commissioned by MI5 or MI6.

Put yourself in Diana's shoes back then – you're told that your private secretary and your ex-police officer have been working against you. It would have made Diana sit back and think, *Well, I wasn't that bad, was I, in 1993, to do what I did?* Patrick says the one thing that annoyed him was that Diana went to her death believing he was corrupt, and that's a difficult thing to live with.

CHAPTER 16

ROS COWARD

'I don't think Charles can do it.'

IN THE AUTUMN of 2021, two Sunday newspapers reported that Michael Fawcett, Prince Charles's former valet, had allegedly offered to arrange an honour for Saudi businessman Mahfouz Marei Mubarak bin Mahfouz, who had donated more than £1.5 million to royal charities. The suggestion that Fawcett had offered these honours in return for financial support to the Prince of Wales's charities is still under investigation. But it was not the first time Fawcett had found himself under intense scrutiny. At the end of the Burrell trial, among the many revelations which spilled out – about George Smith's unhappy life, about Diana's shoddy treatment, and about the practice of staff selling off gifts given to members of the Royal Family – Fawcett resigned as Prince Charles's personal valet, although he remained working for Charles in a different capacity. But the eruption of the cash-for-honours accusation was a reminder of Diana's questions about her husband and his judgement, which she had implicitly asked in the

Martin Bashir interview: how suitable was Prince Charles for the role of the 'top job', as she called it?

Diana's view in the Bashir interview was explicit – she wanted Charles to find peace of mind and 'from that follows other things'. By implication she seemed to want William to be King, not Charles. She was explicit about what she saw as the latter's weaknesses, and suggested he would feel constrained and maybe didn't even want this job, and implied that William would become a much more modern, empathetic, more 'hands on' monarch. In the same interview she had also described how she had included the boys in her charity visits, such as to The Passage homeless project in London, or taken them with her to meet children with terminal illnesses. 'I want them to have an understanding of people's emotions, people's insecurities, people's distress ... I would like a monarchy that has more contact with people.' As for the effect on her boys, she said, 'They have a knowledge – they may not use it, but the seed is there.'

The seed appears to be growing. William, for example, chose to mark his fortieth birthday in June 2022 by selling the *Big Issue*, a publication dedicated to helping the homeless. He spent the day with one of the homeless vendors selling the magazine and, in an accompanying article, spoke of the debt he owed his mother in making him aware of the issues and of wanting to continue her work. Harry, too, with his passion for disabled charities such as the Invictus Games, which he founded, has revealed himself to be carrying on Diana's work. The press often speculates on which parent the boys take after – is William the true inheritor of Charles's identity, and has Harry become the true inheritor of Diana's? Another way in which the couple's disastrous marriage and the struggle between them are still being played out is seen in the division between the two boys, with one alienated from the family, the other with all the family hopes pinned on him. It's the War of the Waleses, as Charles and Diana's marriage came to be dubbed by the media, still being played out, with people still having to position themselves on one side or the other. At a personal level it must be excruciatingly painful for them.

It is interesting that Harry has been ridiculed by some sectors of the British media and pundits like Piers Morgan for those very qualities for which Diana was so admired and which she tried to pass on to her boys. Their wives are dragged in as well to contrast the 'good' and sensible issues with which William gets involved as opposed to the 'mad' ones taken up by Meghan and Harry. Kate is seen as the perfect royal wife while Meghan is often demonised, with their different models of motherhood and wifehood being set against each other. Kate is widely presented as someone who supports William's approach, Meghan often as domineering and controlling of Harry's beliefs.

When I wrote a book about Diana which was focused on her charity work, it was clear that her chosen charities valued her openness about the issues for which Harry is sometimes mocked, particularly those concerned with mental-health issues. They valued her courage in talking to Morton about bulimia and self-harming and suicide attempts – some of the very topics her youngest son now champions.

When Diana died, of course, there was this huge outpouring of appreciation for all the wonderful things she did, and how she's changed for evermore our attitude to mental health. For a long while, when they were not alienated from each other, both William and Harry were doing some very good things with mental health charities and pushing the need for these subjects to be discussed much more openly. But now that Meghan has come on the scene and there is so much press hostility towards her, those important issues have been described as woke, phoney and Californian, a sign of Harry being generally beyond the pale. This is quite shocking because these issues are crucial and deserve more attention, not less.

Diana was remarkable in opening up these issues of mental health even though she was struggling with it herself. Her professionalism towards her charity visits meant she turned up and usually put on an incredible show – giving people her full attention and making it a special day for them – all the while going home to suffer alone with her own issues. From the accounts Morton has given of how *Diana: Her True Story* came to be written, she often went back to Kensington Palace alone and made these recordings, talking explicitly about bulimia and suicidal thoughts. She must have been incredibly lonely, but she gave her all to the charities in the daytime. She was exceptionally dutiful; indeed, driven by duty.

What sort of monarchy Charles or William might offer is more than a question of what sort of personal quirks they display. It's also about how they will manage a very significant move from a matriarchal monarch to a patriarchal one. For seventy years, Queen Elizabeth has to some degree benefited from the perception of female power as softer, less threatening than its male equivalent. The Queen has always been able to draw on the feelings of the mother of the family and, as a result she's always won that respect from people, whether she deserved it or not. These feelings have become much greater recently as she has become older and frailer. Still turning up, still doing her duty, never complaining; she always seems to do the right thing. Some might say the right thing might be to do something in certain situations, but she is not judged for this.

Her role requires absolute discretion and her symbolic position as mother of the nation means that her overlooking of her children's misbehaviour is seen as maternal.

This is a very different reception from the one that Charles is likely to receive, because matriarchal power is not threatening in the way the patriarchal side could be. Because he is a man, expectations will be different about what Charles's power should look like. Will there be a greater general expectation of assertiveness, for example? And, as a consequence, more conflict about any assertive views he offers? He will also carry the complicated personal back story of his relationship with Diana, and all the revelations about his behaviour and lifestyle that subsequently emerged and have been introduced to a whole new generation that watches Netflix's *The Crown*. Charles's apparently more self-indulgent, irascible personality might mean the issue of his suitability for the role reappears, undermining the causes about which he cares passionately.

Meanwhile, the seeds that Diana sowed appear to have fitted William better for this role. His involvement with men's mental health, with child bereavement, with homelessness all suggest he could indeed fulfil Diana's wish for a monarchy 'with more contact with its people' and with a more 'in-depth understanding'.

It's worth bearing in mind Diana's insights about monarchy when considering one of the debates that has raged over her since her death. Was she someone who was manipulated, or did she herself manipulate the press? This is focused particularly around her participation in two key events: the recording of tapes she made for Andrew Morton's book, and her interview with Martin Bashir. Both cases are different. There is no suggestion that Morton manipulated Diana to participate, as Bashir seemingly did. But in both cases Diana used the event constructively, telling not just her story but how such events affect people mentally. She had to use considerable subterfuge for Morton's *Diana: Her True Story*, making secret recordings and sneaking tapes out, or people in, to Kensington Palace. And she was up against the most implacable forces, sometimes talking of the grey men of the establishment who were against her.

The Morton account of how he produced that book really shows how impossibly difficult her life was and how much she desperately wanted her story to be known. She had to go through unbelievable cloak-and-dagger activities to get this message out, much of it about the presence of Camilla in her marriage. She wanted to reveal how cold her marriage was and how unhappy she was – for a Royal to do that, to say that it had taken her to self-harm and bulimia, was remarkable. She was trapped in full public gaze with secrets and lies around her. She didn't really have anyone to support her and there were these two critical moments – the Morton book and the Bashir interview – when she reached out and spoke to the public.

For many women, the story of what happened with Camilla and how it affected Diana's mental health is resonant and will always be: that here was a young woman who was cheated on and then everyone closed ranks and denied that this was happening. Diana was struggling with it on her own, and showed considerable courage in doing what she did. Yet it was never just about her, for she related her story to others suffering from depression, despair and emotional disorders. This was a demonstration of the empathy and intuition, the deep understanding of ordinary people that she thought were necessary for the monarchy to survive. It remains to be seen how that will be viewed in the changing monarchy of the next few years.

CHAPTER 17

KEN WHARFE

*'It's vital the monarchy keeps in touch with
the people – it's what I try to do.'*

IN THE 2022 Netflix documentary, *Jimmy Savile: A Horror Story*, it was revealed that letters were written by Prince Charles to ask Jimmy Savile to help with PR. This astounding revelation raises an important point about whether the 'non-Diana' Royals actually have that much of a grip on the real world. I did know of Savile's connection with Charles and was very suspicious of him anyway purely from a policing standpoint. Savile believed completely in his own importance and confident to do anything he wished – he had the front of Sainsburys and thought he was completely untouchable.

I remember doing an engagement once with Diana and, as we walked along a street, suddenly I heard this voice shouting, 'Now then, everybody, now then, I've got this great lady, young Princess Diana,' and here in front of us was Savile in a turquoise jumpsuit, who had come over a railing to take over. Everyone thought he was a great guy and the fact that he was gatecrashing a royal event was just seen as perfectly acceptable. His personality and sudden unannounced appearance shocked us all, and the local police chief and Lord Lieutenant stared in amazement. Diana of course was amused, as Savile went down on one knee and took her hand. This wasn't part of the reconnaissance, but it nevertheless seemed entertaining – well, for Diana and me at least. The Lord Lieutenant thought otherwise, as his hand grasped the hilt of his ceremonial sword.

The fact of the matter is, the Prince of Wales is rather naive and it's understandable that he thought he could perhaps use Savile to help out. For all I've said about the Prince – and there is a lot of good to him – he is completely unconnected to the real world, or at least he certainly was in the 1980s and 1990s. Back then, and I can see no reason why it will have changed, he often just didn't understand what was happening. He couldn't even understand many of the things his own wife was doing for the betterment of his own children, and his judgement, certainly with people rather than issues, was very clouded. Why would you, as a public figure, want to get involved with an unknown quantity like Savile? People thought he was a gregarious, fun-loving guy with great connections at that time, but we didn't really know anything about him – it was like Diana and her relationship with Al-Fayed when she wanted to use his place in the sun. It may well have suited her, but she didn't think of the bigger picture. What were likely to be the repercussions if things went wrong? What would the fallout be?

The Prince would appear to have written these letters to Savile of his own accord without thinking of the ramifications if things went wrong. Although Savile was a celebrity and was doing such heinous

Above: Diana with her mother, Frances Shand Kydd, at the men's Singles Final, Wimbledon, in July 1993. Ken has said that he would 'count Frances as Diana's best friend'.

Left: Mother and daughter at Charles Spencer's wedding in September 1989. Ken also shared a warm friendship with Frances, and enjoyed staying with her in Scotland.

Left: Diana with Hollie Ann Robinson Marsh, who had lost her hair as a result of chemotherapy, during a visit to Northwick Park Hospital, north-west London, in July 1997, just weeks before her death.

Left: Diana holds two pupils' hands on a visit to a school in Carajas, Brazil, in April 1991. Ken is to her right, and her friend Lucia Flecha da Lima is behind her.

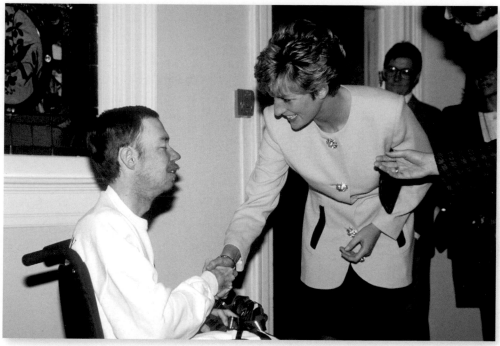

Above: Diana shakes hands with a patient at the Casey House Aids Hospice in Toronto, Canada, October 1991. At the time AIDS was all too often regarded as a 'gay plague', so her work in raising awareness about it was ground-breaking.

Below left: Diana wearing body armour at a minefield being cleared by the Halo Trust in Huambo, Angola, January 1997. As with AIDS, her very public support for anti-landmine initiatives was invaluable.

Below right: Diana, in a pale blue shalwar kameez, cradles a young cancer patient during a visit to a hospital in Lahore, Pakistan, in February 1996.

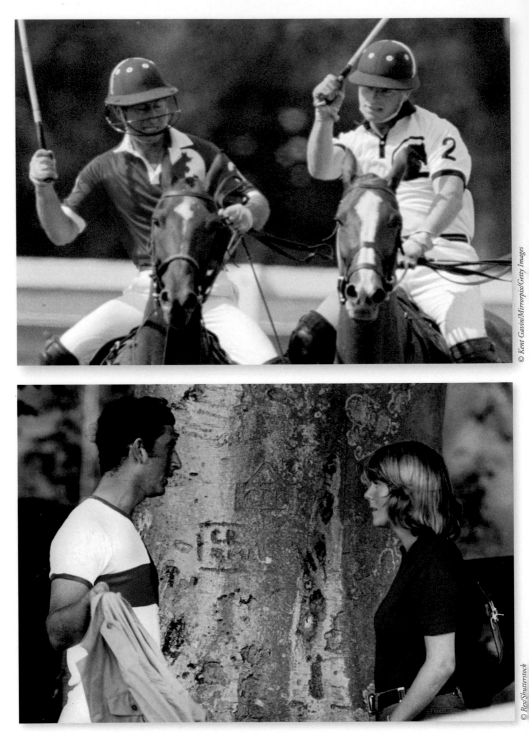

Above: Prince Charles (left) and Major James Hewitt during a polo match in July 1991; according to Ken, 'Diana's affair with Hewitt undoubtedly brought her some pleasure.'

Below: Charles talking to Camilla Parker Bowles during a polo match in July 1975, six years before his marriage to Diana.

Above: The famous image of Diana alone in front of the Taj Mahal in Agra, India, in February 1992. The marble mausoleum holds the tomb of the Mughal emperor Shah Jahan's favourite wife. Charles was at another engagement – as metaphors for an unhappy marriage go, the photograph takes a lot of beating.

Below: Diana during her interview with Martin Bashir for the BBC's *Panorama* progamme, November 1995. It has subsequently emerged that she was manipulated into giving the interview, but its effects were far-reaching.

Above left: Hasnat Khan, the heart surgeon with whom Diana had a two-year relationship that he ended in June 1997; she was, by all accounts, deeply in love with him.

Above right: Diana and William (with his hand over his face) holidaying with Dodi Fayed at St-Tropez in the South of France, July 1997.

Below: Diana on holiday in the Virgin Islands in April 1990. Ken would often arrange for a press photo shoot in return for their leaving the Princess alone for the rest of her trip.

Above: Diana's coffin, borne by eight pallbearers from the Welsh Guards, is carried into Westminster Abbey before her funeral, 6 September 1997. In the foreground, tributes from the public throng the railings and pavement.

Below: From left to right: Earl Spencer, Prince William, Prince Harry and Prince Charles in Diana's funeral cortège – her brother, her sons and their father united in mourning.

A portrait of Diana by the late French fashion photographer Patrick Demarchelier.
The Princess gave this print to Ken when he told her how much he liked it.

things which we found out after his death, his status endeared him to other celebrities, as it was good for both sides.

I wonder to what extent, if any, did Charles's own private office intervene? Perhaps not at all, since he was prone to writing letters off his own bat, as he did with Savile, and they would have gone without any scrutiny from his own staff, which is slightly worrying. It is, again, the naivete of it all which has to be questioned; what did he think he could get from using the services of Savile in this way? It is worrying to consider, especially when you consider Andrew's recent behaviour in escorting his mother to the memorial event for his father in such a public way. Why is there no one giving appropriate advice? Or if advice is given, it is being ignored on occasion. Andrew will honestly feel he has the right to be a public Royal. Again, it is just not reading the line properly and this is where Diana was much better – she was more streetwise and she understood it better; the others don't, they think they can just move on when they've had enough of things, controversial or not.

We rightly live in a very transparent society but the Royals just don't seem to get that. Personally, I feel that if Andrew had to be at the memorial service, he should have been one of the general congregation and made a dignified, low-key entrance – holding up his mother in front of the world was not that. I can understand the Queen may have wanted such a public statement but even she must have thought, *Is this good for me, for my son, for the public?* Irrespective of what your children do, do you still, as a mother, always love them, even when it has been alleged that they have been involved in such heinous behaviour? In these circumstances, given her frailty, was it right for Andrew to show his face at the Remembrance Service for his father? It may have been the only opportunity. There had to be a reason for him to be there and escorting his mother was the only reason – that must have been of her doing.

Andrew is so arrogant that he believes because the money has been paid to Virginia Giuffre, he can now return to normal public life as the case is done, it's finished, it's over, he's back. He will honestly believe that, I feel. There was a great deal of negative fallout for what should have been a very positive reflection of the life of the Duke of Edinburgh, a man we all know had stood by the Queen's side for seventy-two years. Instead, the event focused entirely on Andrew and whether he should or should not have been there. No matter – the damage is done. The Royal Family and their advisors were wrong, but my guess is that Andrew would have run the show on that one; whatever anybody said, he would have been in there. Many of us have heard that he's the Queen's favourite, but I can't, for the life of me, think why – he's made some incredible blunders in his life, one of which, it could be argued, was marrying Sarah Ferguson.

Diana was, eventually, rightly worried about her association with Fergie, which meant that, thankfully, their relationship waned considerably.

In my view, Fergie, whose own marriage was collapsing and knew well the problems of Diana's, was trying to encourage the latter to leave at the same time as she did, thus allowing her to blame the Firm. I did say to Diana, 'Just be careful, because it may appear to be genuine but I believe she's doing it for her own self-interest. Her public approval ratings are so low and one way to raise them is for you to come on board. There's no reason why you should – what's in it for you? You have to think like that in life, Ma'am. "What's in it for me?" There's totally nothing in it for you – you have to pull out.' She actually did listen, and she did distance herself from her sister-in-law.

On that subject about advising and talking to people, it's very like the letters I received from Frances Shand Kydd – what was the point of them? Diana would relay things to her mother and her mother would come back to me – because actually, courtiers don't really want to get involved in deep matters of advice, they're there to advise on matters of official policy but when it comes down to being deeply personal, it can backfire. If you say something they like, fine, but if you say something they don't like, you have a problem. I remember speaking to Patrick Jephson about this. He would perhaps say, 'If you get a chance, could you discuss this issue with Diana on the way to Highgrove?' That really wasn't my area, but I didn't have a problem with it if it helped him as we worked as a team, and it cut both ways. There were times I would say things to Diana that she wouldn't particularly like and I'd get frozen out for a while, but I wasn't employed by her, I was employed by the Commissioner and if I did go, I wouldn't be without a job. That wasn't the case with courtiers so their role was very different.

It's very much the same within the Prince of Wales's office. I wonder if he'd said, 'I'm going to write to Jimmy Savile,' would anyone have said he shouldn't? Knowing the sycophancy of them, I can just imagine them saying, 'Oh, I think that's a very good idea, Sir, I'm sure he would be delighted to hear from you.'

Sometimes with Patrick, if there was a difficult subject, both of us would play it in the hope that there would be a chance of winning. What Patrick was saying was usually sound, but it wasn't as easy for him as it was for me sitting in the front of a car driving somewhere.

Patrick was only ever engaged with Diana in official duties, whether in the office or on a public engagement. Sitting in a car with someone, completely away from everybody, going down the M4 – well, it's amazing what you talk about, and I had that with Diana.

Of course, one of the things she often spoke about was the affair between her husband and 'his lady'. She was particularly hurt by the friends of Charles who completely colluded in his affair with Camilla. There were many 'safe' houses for Charles and Camilla; I didn't know where they were but it was an open secret. My own boss, Chief Superintendent Colin Trimming, should have been told everything in a normal business, but neither of us could really tell the other anything as we were in a unique situation. He was anxious to find out more about what Diana was doing so he could report back to the Prince and others, but Diana knew there were safe houses and places they would meet, and she didn't want anyone to know what *she* knew.

It was terribly convoluted. The Prince had a huge coterie of friends that he could use, some that Diana knew, some that she didn't. The friendship, the camaraderie, within his own circle of friends was very powerful. People like Nicholas Soames and other titled friends could offer up their houses for the liaison to continue in the way that it did. Diana was completely aware of that, but there was nothing she could do about it. If she were to know about it, what would it achieve by broaching it? All that it would bring would be an argument, and it would go nowhere. It was difficult for me with Trimming on a lot of occasions, not that I ever asked him what was going on with Camilla. To be fair, Diana never asked me that. He would never have told me anyway – but he did continue to try and prise things out of me.

'Don't ask me, Colin, I won't tell you.'

'Come on, Wharfie, you know where I'm at.'

'I know exactly where you're at!'

If we went on holiday, he'd be keen to know who was going but I'd openly say, 'It's got nothing to do with you.'

'It's got everything to do with me. I'm your line manager.' That always came into the matter and I learned to live with it. Colin was a friend and socially, we were very good friends. To his credit, he accepted my position and tried to pull it back a little.

Camilla still retains her house in Ray Mill, which is not too far from Highgrove. I have no idea what Charles and Camilla's living arrangements are at Clarence House. It has always struck me that theirs is a fairly unusual relationship, but they are both very good at performing on stage. Whatever happens behind the scenes, where they have fairly independent lifestyles, is less clear, but as a double act, in the public eye, they appear to be a good show. We know now that Camilla will be Queen within the next few years and strong rumours suggest they will move into Windsor Castle as I don't think Charles particularly wants Buckingham Palace. He and Camilla are not completely independent; they just have a lifestyle that seems different from 'normal' relationships, whatever 'normal' may be. If you compare their marriage to that of William and Kate, there is a massive generational difference. The very fact that Camilla still retains her property in Wiltshire, which is not far from Highgrove, is just how they 'run' their relationship.

A great friend of mine worked for Camilla with his wife when he left the police. She became Camilla's estate manager and he was something of an odd-job and security man. He spent a lot of time there and he found her style rather difficult. One day, she said to him, 'Will you have a look at the swimming pool. It needs cleaning. Perhaps you would like to do it?'

He discovered a leak that needed immediate repair work, so he rang around to find out the daily rate he should charge to fix it. He found out it was about £25 an hour to clean the pool and that someone professional needed to look at the leak.

Camilla exclaimed, 'Twenty-five pounds! My goodness me, twenty-five pounds!'

She then spoke to the Prince's Private Secretary, who summoned him to London.

'I gather you've been having a chat with the Duchess about the swimming pool?'

'That's right, Sir, yes.'

'Twenty-five pounds is an awful lot of money, don't you think?'

'No, I don't think it is. I've checked, and that's the going rate.'

The Private Secretary pondered this, and then asked him, 'Have you ever heard of what they call "mates' rates"?'

'I'm sorry, Sir?'

'Mates' rates. You know …'

'Well, yes, Sir, but Mrs Parker Bowles is not a "mate" of mine, Sir.'

She never did look after that pool and, some years later, was landed with a multi-thousand-pound repair bill. This is so typical of how they work, it's quite extraordinary. They certainly have a very different style of life to most people.

I think when Diana said, 'There were three of us in this marriage,' it was totally honest, real gutsy stuff. This was the basis of the decline in her marriage – it wasn't just that the Prince was having a fling with someone occasionally. Camilla was there continuously, certainly towards the end of Diana's life. Three of them in the marriage was never workable. What happened at the party held by Camilla's sister, Annabel Elliot, was bad enough, but it wasn't just that occasion. It was that the entire period before and after that marriage was part of it. It took Diana ten years of her life to answer the question, 'How will I let people know about my problem?' Up until that point, everyone was saying she was paranoid and therefore writing her off, as the Prince of Wales's camp and circle of friends was so much more powerful in terms of representing his best interests. Diana's best interests, though, were not in any way defended. Even when she went to the Queen and asked for help. I think the Queen was probably right to say something along the lines of, 'Hang on, this isn't my problem – you need to speak to your husband about this.'

'Ha! That's the problem – he won't talk about it!'

Even Diana's own mother had said to her, 'Can't you just speak to him?'

'No, I can't!' said Diana.

A combination of the couple's separation, the Morton book, and the Bashir interview brought the divorce about, but I still think Diana was very brave to say what she said. Like many people, I was shocked that she gave the interview to Bashir, but with hindsight, what other options were available for her to put her story out there? It's a really sad case that one has to negotiate with a journalist to do that – although Bashir started those negotiations with her brother and suggested that there were spies within her own camp and this prompted her without reservations to give the interview. I don't think this was just at the time of Bashir; I think it had been brewing for years, whether through her own paranoia or through friends.

Diana believed she was being bugged – Fergie got involved in that she sent a team of so-called experts from Sussex to debug Diana's apartment. In the end, they were arrested because they didn't have the proper authority and went in there under the pretext of being carpet cleaners. I don't think the Duchess of York was exactly helpful. Diana didn't know how to solve the 'problem' of being bugged and Fergie, in her inimitable way, said, 'I have people who can do that.' So somehow these people were allowed to enter Kensington Palace under the pretext of cleaning Diana's carpets. After a while, the idiots walked into the police control room and asked about the line from Diana's room.

'Who are you?' they were asked. 'Aren't you carpet cleaners?'

They owned up pretty quickly, and the four of them were detained. That was a blunder Fergie caused, but I don't know what the fallout was for Diana. Her apartment was checked out properly and no devices were found at all. It was an ongoing issue for her, however. I don't think when I was there it was so bad, but Diana's close friend, James Colthurst has told me that she believed it was true, that she was being bugged – but what would be the reason? For me, the worrying thing was that the 'carpet cleaners' had been allowed access within a secure perimeter.

I never felt any concern that Diana was being bugged because I had no evidence of it, but her behaviour was very strange in 1993. There were people who, whether they had good or bad intentions, were telling her to be careful.

Immediately she'd say, 'What do you mean?'

'Just be careful.'

'Why?'

'Well – you never know.'

'What? What don't I know?'

'Things. There could be things ...'

It was all very vague but played into any concerns she had. Mara Berni, the owner of Diana's favourite restaurant San Lorenzo, who was very dramatic, was always saying to her in her broken English: 'You have to be careful with everybody. You don't know who they all are.'

'What do you mean by that?'

'Well, you know, just be careful. I have a very good friend – she can read you.'

Then along came the Tarot card readers and psychics who Diana thought could break down her fear, but instead they wrote pages of absolute drivel about how 'there could be dark forces but you'll be fine because you're an honest person'. Diana believed all of this – that was the problem. It was tragic.

Diana was right in every way about Charles and Camilla – the bugging was another matter, but she had a right to fear she might be. Everyone knew that Diana knew about Camilla, even Charles knew it. Everyone knew about Camilla and that he didn't want to lose her. They would be asking, what will Diana do next? Is she going to do anything stupid? They obviously believed she could. The relationship with Charles and Camilla was never going to break down – quite how they thought that relationship would play itself out, I have no idea. It's always been my firm belief that, had Diana not died in a car crash in Paris, but was divorced – which would have happened – I am not sure Charles's relationship with Camilla would have ended in marriage. If Diana was still alive, that would have confirmed in every respect what he had tried to ignore and what she had told the world about. Publicly, it would never have worked for the Prince. I don't think he and Camilla would ever have married.

Diana was absolutely right about the relationship throughout her life. The sad thing was, I don't think there was a day that went by, from 1981, when she wasn't concerned with the Camilla issue and trying to work out a solution with damage limitation – although as the years went on, I don't think she cared about damage limitation. Somehow the true facts of her marriage had to be revealed. She had the trump card. I don't think anybody suspected she would engage herself with Morton, that was a huge shock to everyone. For the second explosion to come through Bashir – that wasn't expected either. They were dealing with an unknown quantity now. It could have been so different if they'd listened, but they felt it wasn't in their best interests, that ultimately a divorce would happen and that would be an end to it. What they didn't know was that Diana's life would end in Paris – no one could have predicted that.

CHAPTER 18

ROS COWARD

*'People think that at the end of the day,
a man is the only answer. Actually, a fulfilling
job is better for me.'*

THE CONNECTION BETWEEN Prince Charles and the disgraced television presenter Jimmy Savile is undeniably unfortunate. The prolific paedophile cosied up to many personalities and famous people and not a few were taken in by his over-familiarity and apparent childishness. But the degree to which Prince Charles was taken in was surprising. Diana too had dealings with Savile – he invited her to charity events and, even though there was no intimacy, he acted as though he were close to her. Prince Charles, however, actually asked Jimmy Savile to help him with publicity and PR matters. More surprising, he also asked him for advice on how to deal with certain more personal matters, at one point suggesting that Savile might talk to Sarah Ferguson, whose behaviour at the time was seen as causing concern.

Although there were rumours, few knew Savile was a paedophile at that point, but he was certainly a strange, somewhat repellent character. It seems extraordinary that anyone in the Royal Family might have asked him to help them sort out their public image, or give them advice on attending the correct events to win popularity. Even more surprising was that Charles would turn to someone like Savile to help with understanding what might help their popularity when Diana was already part of the team. She unquestionably had the popular touch, yet Charles chose to reach out to someone like Savile as though he had the answer. Was this failure to utilise Diana's talents because some in royal circles resented her popularity? And if so, did this resentment indicate an absolute failure to grasp her potential, to make use of her character and talent?

Diana's was a dazzling personality. She was charismatic and beautiful, and she was open and compassionate. But the source of her popularity was an ability to connect with people in a genuine and authentic way. Despite any negative commentary, no one ever suggested she was phoney in those public interactions, which included her connection with people at the end of their lives, some of whom were dying in extreme situations. The Royals didn't understand this ability to connect, especially with marginal groups such as AIDS sufferers. When Diana spoke to these people she often talked about herself, showing that she could relate their suffering to hers in some way and vice versa; which is true empathy – the ability to understand and share another's feelings. She was open about her situation to people. Yet there were frequently hints from royal courtiers or media commentators, often a suggestion that she shouldn't be doing that, she shouldn't be openly sharing so much, whether to journalists or to people she met through charities.

Some aspects of that emotional openness did have difficult consequences. In the case of the Bashir interview, it seems Diana was manipulated into believing people were spying on her, with damaging consequences for her mental health, but she wanted to communicate with not just her immediate circle, but with the wider public. She was mocked for saying she wanted to talk to 'the people' and for suggesting those same people understood her. Some said she should not have spoken, that she should have been a more dutiful wife and that she would have been more powerful as a result. And, indeed, later, that she would still have been alive.

But what is it that the critics think Diana should have been? Since her extraordinary talent was to reach out and communicate, that's what made the connection, but it was something that challenged the establishment. People felt they knew her – she even followed up on meetings, checking in with those who were dying or otherwise facing huge challenges. Even the fact that she said she didn't need a man to feel complete was such a reversal of traditional ideals of female royalty that it was astonishing.

There are plenty of commentators and biographers who have not really approached Diana's life very empathetically. They've judged her as if she was a powerful, manipulative woman, and also someone driven by emotional disturbance. They haven't really looked at the situation she was in as a young woman trying to create some kind of meaningful life in very strange circumstances. Increasingly she was alone, whether by choice or necessity. She was dealing with powerful people and organisations largely on her own, and there were even active briefings against her from the 'other side'. The battle for public sympathy wasn't called the War of the Waleses for nothing. Until and after the divorce, many of the Prince's friends were speaking about her to the press. For her part, she was just a woman on her own with very little support;

she didn't have a legion of brand and reputation managers. She was the most famous woman in the world, yet she was trying to lead a relatively ordinary life in a wildly extraordinary situation. When people say she was manipulative, they need to remember this: she was exceptional in many ways, but she was also a very young woman learning how to make a life.

Much of the commentary on Diana has been written by men who seem to forget these facts. I wonder if people will look back historically and see a young woman who has been defined by the male gaze and by male interpretations. They might wonder about the amount of effort these critics have put into trying to prove that Diana was paranoid or mentally unstable, and somehow the architect of her own fate. Diana never did much 'wrong', but she is often judged as though she had. Someone like Fergie was much more in the mould of current celebrities in that she appears to have been more materialistic and more likely to have used her position to generate an income. Diana never did that, she was quite modest in her aspirations. Her personal style wasn't a glitzy one, and in spite of the descriptions of her as unstable, she kept up appearances at public engagements, and rarely let her personal feelings dominate the occasions.

In terms of the affairs, another source of criticisms, Diana was a beautiful woman in her thirties, neglected by her husband who was having a long-term affair, and she desperately wanted a relationship and a sex life. What is so awful about that? She had been flung into this marriage at nineteen years old, had grown up in the public eye and was coming into herself. The lack of empathy in some of these judgements is ironic given that she was so empathetic herself. The commentary is also harsh in trying to establish that last period of her life as fearful, paranoid and manipulative, but another version is to see that she was trying to become herself in very difficult circumstances in which some people were against her. She was trying to reach out.

Twenty-five years after Diana's death, evidence is still emerging about why her situation was so difficult. The allegation that Michael Fawcett may have been offering an honour in exchange for a donation to Charles's charity has again seemingly torn back the veil on the strange world she was forced to inhabit, a world which is more complicated and sometimes less honourable than it claims to be. This is precisely what the Paul Burrell trial also revealed: the existence of a not terribly honourable world that surrounded Diana. What came out during that trial, and in the revelations which flowed out subsequently, was how she was generally treated and ostracised while the establishment, critical of her behaviour, themselves inhabited a world of the strangest expectations.

There are so many things that would just never have come out – many intimate details, what she was fearful of, how people behaved around her – were it not for the Burrell trial, which brought all this before the public. The evidence given at the beginning of the trial before it was abandoned purported to show how her family treated Diana. The Spencers had to take the stand, and some of what came out seemed shocking. Even her own family were accused of making her life difficult and not having her interests at heart. The defence that Burrell used was that they hadn't really cared about her and that her mother had shouted at her on the phone about her Muslim boyfriends, and her sister had fobbed off the godchildren with second-hand broken gifts. There were also revelations that Charles Spencer had offered

Diana a bolthole on the Althorp Estate and then withdrawn it, which left her devastated. The legal strategy was to justify Burrell's appropriation of Diana's belongings by undermining the credibility of the Spencers who had, until that point, largely been seen as the upholders of Diana's memory. Frances Shand Kydd and Diana's sister, Sarah had initially supported Paul Burrell and employed him at the Diana, Princess of Wales Memorial Fund, but they fell out, allegedly because of a number of bad judgements on Burrell's side. He had turned against them and his evidence painted the Spencers as the family which let Diana down in those last years. When the trial was abandoned, the British media immediately went into a state where they were inundated with leaks about what Burrell had been going to use to defend himself, a lot of which was evidence about the Spencers.

But while the evidence against the Spencers may have seemed damning, what emerged through the leaks about Charles's courtiers and their impact on Diana's life was much more shocking. It was through the Burrell trial, in particular its abandonment and the subsequent leaks to the press, that the public came to hear of a missing tape on which Diana had recorded the words of George Smith alleging to have been raped by a male courtier.

Diana felt that this hadn't been investigated properly. The Peat Report into what had really happened to some extent reproduced the dismissive response to these accusations. The report, like the officials to whom George Smith had originally complained, decided that the allegation had always been absurd, not worth investigating. Diana, however, was inclined to think these allegations were not absurd, because she thought that the world the courtiers inhabited was not healthy.

Poor George Smith died in sad circumstances, having possibly drunk himself to death, so no one will ever know the truth about his allegations, but the saga has relevance to Diana's life. This was the kind of world she felt she was moving in. Her detractors would say the whole affair was her stirring up something that had nothing to do with her, and that she shouldn't have stuck her nose in. However, these courtiers were having a significant influence on her life at the time, seemingly preventing her from making the situation with Charles any easier. The incident certainly indicates that she was paranoid about what was going on.

Once the Burrell trial ended, the defence was leaked and a lot of journalists began to sniff around the George Smith story. Burrell was spirited away; he went quiet and didn't tell anyone what he was doing for six months. He was in fact writing his memoirs, from which the main revelation to emerge was about Diana's relationship with the heart surgeon Hasnat Khan. Burrell's memoirs give an intimate account of those last years of her life but they were full of teases and hints at secrets still to be revealed, many of which seem to have been fabricated. Called *A Royal Duty* and published in 2003, the book was called by Princes William and Harry 'a cold and overt betrayal' of their mother.

Burrell may have described himself as Diana's rock, the only keeper of her secrets, but that is most certainly something which can be challenged. If he was one of the significant elements in her life, there is always a question as to whether he was ever dependable. Might he have been manipulating Diana for his own ends? He was, no doubt, present in her life but was an unreliable guardian. In those last few years, she had so little around her that was solid.

People often forget that in the last year of her life, Diana made those trips to Angola and Bosnia, which were significant interventions, not least because they highlighted her determination to do something about the blight of landmines. When I interviewed Bill Deedes, the former editor of the *Daily Telegraph*, who went on the trip with Diana, it was clear that he had been genuinely incredibly impressed by her. He said that her bravery and interaction with people were astonishing. He went on to say, 'She wasn't a saint or a sinner – she was a human being. A complex one, an interesting one, and everyone is trying to make her one or the other.'

In her last years, the props that she was leaning on proved to be rotten, and the Diana we thought we knew from her public persona was a woman desperately trying to make a version of herself that she could live with, a spirit that could flourish and thereby pave the way to a new life.

CHAPTER 19

KEN WHARFE

'I will fight for my children on any level so they can reach their potential as human beings, and in their public duties.'

WHEN YOU SEE how William has carved his life out with his children, it's an exact replica of the world he had as a child: the same sort of school, the same style of raising his children, keeping them out of the public eye but also introducing them to a way of life that is a combination of some normality and privilege – and Diana laid the foundations for that.

On the rare times we see William with his children there does seem to be a genuine warmth, and he got that from his mother, far less so than his father. The Prince did acknowledge, very early on, that the style his wife had brought to the table with the children was probably the right one. Despite their own unhappiness, I never witnessed on any occasion William or Harry being affected by the marriage. It was never allowed to take place in front of them. There were so many other players in their lives, the staff who had an almost parental role to give them some freedom and fun, and it worked.

Charles and Diana were unhappy as adults, but they never allowed it to filter to the children and I think they were blissfully unaware of it all. Even people like Camilla and James Hewitt would just have been seen as friends of Mum and Dad when they were around. Later on, when the boys realised their parents were separated, most of their friends would have that sort of family set-up too, so I don't think it really mattered in that sense.

Certainly, throughout the junior stage of their lives, Diana was very instrumental in being there as much as she could, trying to do normal things and even openly encouraging the kids to go and stay with friends. There were occasions when they were old enough to have sleepovers, and other children would be invited back to the Palace. On holidays, Diana would say, 'Do you want to bring a friend with you?' Some child would get a great holiday in the Caribbean, all expenses paid, and that was through the generosity of Diana. She was keen to break away from the traditions of royalty, where education and some upbringing was involved. What we see now is that William, and I daresay Harry, will use the template of their mother.

I don't think Diana was ever told 'no' about any of this. I don't think she was ever told, 'Look, there are boundaries here and you can't go beyond that.' I think she was strong on this, she stood firm. Initially, the Prince of Wales was apprehensive at where they were about to be educated as it didn't suit with what he had experienced, but he never jumped in with both feet; he was often prepared to see how things panned out and he could see it worked for the boys. The media never criticised their style of education – they praised Diana for breaking with tradition and it captured a great deal of support. Charles acknowledged after two or three years, it wasn't a bad idea, it was working. Diana was insistent that, from thereon in, the senior stage of education should be somewhat different and it was unlikely she'd send the boys to a local grammar school – it would have to continue in the traditional way and Sandhurst was the natural choice simply because her brother had been there, her father likewise. Being Royal, by virtue of duty, it was obvious that the boys would have to go to a military academy because of their titles. Once the pre-preparatory and preparatory schools were out of the way, it was agreed that Sandhurst and Eton were the only preferred options.

Weekends at Kensington Palace, or even Highgrove, were noisy, family events. The household generally made it work, and they weren't weekends for the faint-hearted at times. They had a swimming pool which was often used, and I even remembering Diana once ordering a truckload of playpit balls. Everybody was expected to be part of weekends of fun. When the Prince wasn't there, she would encourage all members of staff to use the pool, which was a complete anathema to Charles. It wound him up a great deal and boiled over into the unacceptable as far as he was concerned. To him, Diana was losing sight of who she was – there are things that Royals do and things that Royals do not do; there are things that the staff do and things the staff should not do under any circumstances. Diana broke tradition in that respect – she thought, if it was available and didn't hurt anyone, why not let everyone be together and use the facilities? There were weekend BBQs which she encouraged the staff to attend, thinking up menus the kids would like – but the Prince would never do things like that. He was never discourteous or impolite with the staff – on the contrary, in fact, but there was a 'them and us' situation and you knew exactly where you stood. With Diana, there was always an edge. You could find yourself, if not careful, overstepping because of the environment she encouraged. This was her style and everyone, without fail, would have worked continuously for her if asked. At the end of an eight-hour shift, if she wanted the staff to stay another six hours, they wouldn't question it. They enjoyed working for her a great deal. It was that simple.

She had many birthday parties for the boys – those were big events. I remember when William was very keen on Thomas the Tank Engine and the chef made a cake to reflect that. She would have huge parties where everyone was invited, the staff as well as William and Harry's peer group. She had a fairness with the boys, and the distribution of love and gifting was very equal. They were invited back to their friends' houses, that was something she allowed. It was quite the thing to take children on their birthdays off to a burger bar or a pizza place rather than to their houses, and she was happy for that to happen for William and Harry too. Bill Wyman's Sticky Fingers restaurant in Kensington High Street became a regular destination for trips, as well as parties.

On the way back home, Diana would often ask William and Harry, 'What would you like for supper?'

William would invariably say, 'I'd love some sausages,' and we'd go to Marks & Spencer in Kensington High Street. They loved all that. There were the best chefs you could think of back home, but they wanted the normal life of popping into a shop to pick up some sausages. They didn't see anything unusual in it apart from the odd person looking at them, but they learned to live with that. I think Diana enjoyed it. Yes, there was recognition of who she was, you couldn't fail to recognise her – and added to that was me or my colleagues loitering behind shelves, trying to give her as much privacy as possible! It wasn't always easy, but I think it was a good education for them. It was a fashionable part of London, but they were still seeing real life.

By contrast, I remember on one occasion getting back to Kensington Palace to be met by Charles.

'Where have you been?' he asked.

'Papa, we've been to an amazing burger bar, then we went to Marks & Spencer! It was great!'

He looked at Diana and said, 'Why in the world did you take them to a *burger bar*? We have perfectly good chefs, they can make you amazing burgers.'

'Oh come on, Charles! It's a fun day out!'

'But why?'

He just couldn't understand it. He couldn't see why she would want to do it. They had a mini brigade of chefs, including the top pasta chef from Italy who came via Antonio Carluccio, there were young chefs who were brilliant, but when her boys wanted sausages from M&S, that's what Diana got them! She would write in the menu book quite frequently – she didn't want weekly suggestions of French delights, a menu even written in French. She would often strike through suggestions and write 'BJP (baked jacket potato) x2 plus beans'! Fish fingers for William and Harry were an oft-requested item. This was the difference with her. Kids of any age rarely want properly prepared meals, they want other things – eating is often an inconvenience and being Royal didn't change that for Harry and William. William liked chicken and rice, he dined out on that for a long time, whereas Diana's favourite was a baked jacket potato with cheese and onion. When friends came round, the chefs came into their own – I have a menu book which shows what she did with their suggestions and that always entertained me.

Most of the trips to a shop were split-second decisions but it was never a problem, no one was forewarned we were coming. We got to know the staff at the Sticky Fingers restaurant; there was maybe the odd photographer who turned up and Diana acknowledged that. She didn't like it, but there wasn't much she could do about it; there wasn't much I could do about it either. I could only police it in a way that wasn't aggressive – I would send him across to a doorway, say he could get a picture when we came out, and ask politely not to see him again. They bought that. It would be very different now – everyone today is a potential paparazzi, many pictures taken now are provided by those on the street with their iPhones, and Diana would have been at the mercy of that. There was a picture recently of the Queen on a walkabout when a ten-year-old boy asked for a selfie on his phone, which breaks just about every rule there is!

The press in my opinion never posed a threat in terms of Diana's life, although she found it an inconvenience, but she also accepted it was part of being a princess and learned to live with it. There were good days and bad days, but I have to say the bad days were rare.

The parents from school and the ones I met when I took the boys to friends' houses were unfazed by it all. They were discreet, some titled, and completely unaware of Diana and indeed of the state of her marriage. She was one of them, a nice person, jolly and generous. Everything was normal in that sense – there was almost a neighbourly attitude among school families. The boys had a lot, but Diana was very keen they weren't flooded out with gifts. Birthdays were different but there were no mini-Ferraris purchased.

On the day itself, all of these presents would turn up, but like all children, by the following afternoon, they'd be playing with the cardboard boxes or asking the chefs or any other willing member of staff to play with them. They weren't overindulged with presents – she wanted them to be good people, not indulged little monsters. The Harrods green van used to turn up fairly regularly with gifts for the children and Diana, and in the end she gave instructions that the driver was just to turn around and go back. Mohamed Al-Fayed soon got the message. She saw the dangers of that. She was fairly streetwise, and I often wondered where she got that from. She knew how things ticked in that area of London.

There were gift lists for birthdays and Christmas but they weren't over-generous. I don't remember massive presents, mostly things they could use and play with outside, such as the ball pit and they had countless books and videos. When people came round, Diana would say, 'Please, they have enough, they don't need anything else – just turn up, just bring yourselves.' People understood that.

She was very keen not to spoil them in that sense. 'They have enough fun in their lives anyway because of who they are,' she would say. 'They have houses everywhere, friends who have all the trappings, they don't lack for things.' Interestingly, I never heard William or Harry say they were bored, probably because there was so much activity all the time. Sometimes they'd burst in and say, 'Any chance we can play football, Ken?'

'Give me ten minutes,' I'd reply.

It would be Harry who would complain about that ten-minute wait. He was always very impatient. One day he asked me, 'Can you send me on a radio mission?'

I gave him my radio and said, 'Go to the kitchen and speak to the chef and call me. Then go to the chauffeur and I'll give you another message.'

Off he went while I worked. Eventually he asked, 'Is it all right if I go round to Aunt Jane's?' That was Diana's sister who lived just out of the gate at Kensington Palace, in the Old Barracks. I rang Jane to check it was okay if Harry popped round as he wanted something to do.

'Yes, of course – send him down and I'll stand outside until he gets here.'

I telephoned the police immediately, 'Harry's going down to Jane Fellowes. Can you supervise his walk to Lady Jane Fellowes, please?'

Off he went with his radio in his khaki army kit uniform, which he was never out of. Half an hour later, Jane told me, 'He's on his way back.'

'He's on his way up to you,' I told the police officers on duty.

Ten minutes later, there was no sign. I radioed him. 'Harry, it's Ken – where are you?'

'Just a moment,' he said. 'I'm outside Tower Records!' Tower Records in Kensington High Street – Christ! What the hell was he doing there?

I ran out of my office and ran all the way there to see this small boy in army fatigues with my radio, standing in a shop doorway. That was one of the few times I had a small panic. When I think back, that was rather serious. Jane had let him out the door, thinking he would head straight back to Kensington Palace, but he had decided he would do something else, took a left turn and off he went. He was only six or seven years old at the time. Their childhood was fun, there's no doubt about that.

In all honesty, I think colleagues of mine have overplayed problems with the press. When I finished working with Diana, I headed up the Close Protection Team and I wouldn't have this war against the media. They're just doing their job, why give them a bad time? All that's needed is a way to deal with a problem if one of them *becomes* a problem. I think there is a sense of loyalty that once one of the photographers knows something is about to happen, they tip off their friends. I knew that once a particular journalist was in the loop, they'd all know, and the media would be there. They even got us at Heathrow when we were going out on trips as they'd check the flights and the passenger lists. That sort of thing never bothered me. If you stuck to a format, all they wanted was a photograph, so why not give them one? They wanted downtime too – they didn't want to work all day, they wanted one decent photograph or one story to please their editor and that was that. I'd find an opportunity to give them a picture if Diana was prepared to do it – she wasn't always, but she realised at some point she had to, as it was in her interests anyway.

In those early days, she did enjoy being photographed with the children. We'd go to Cirencester unannounced, but shopkeepers would tip off the media and it was just the way of it. She got a bit of a kick out of doing normal things alone with her children, knowing that it was something her husband the Prince would never do. Diana was very against him going hunting with the boys, she was against blood sports and there was also always a risk Camilla would be there. She particularly didn't enjoy the pheasant shoots at Sandringham. She understood the shooting, I think, but hated the absolute destruction of wildlife, many of whom weren't destroyed outright and struggled on for a while before dying. She found that very difficult. She never won that case and William and Harry did shoot. They'd find it difficult to continue to do that now in terms of the public view.

As she was a mother, I'm not certain Diana lost many battles. She was always fearful because of the situation with her own marriage and where divorce was an inevitability, what would the Queen or the monarchy do to her children? She had a fear they would be 'taken away', but I think what would have been more likely is that she would have been allowed limited access. I can't honestly see why that would have happened in a modern monarchy, but she did fear it. She was consciously or subconsciously modernising the Royals anyway and I don't think that this fear they would be taken away would happen. I don't think the boys would have allowed it, they loved her so much.

She did have the lion's share of the custody when the separation happened in 1992 – before that, they had agreed a format where they each had the children every other weekend. However, the Prince acknowledged when that began, both of the boys were far happier with Diana, as she could provide and arrange events he could not. As young boys, they wanted to be where the action was. I remember one winter, Diana taking William and Harry plus invited friends to Playscape Racing in the old Clapham bus garage, a go-karting experience in south London which Diana enjoyed too.

'What do you think, Ken? Any chance Martin [Howell, the circuit owner] would bring a couple of go-karts to Highgrove to have a party on the estate?'

It wasn't a problem and Martin duly brought four the following weekend – the Prince thankfully was away, he would never have allowed such a thing. A circuit was set up in the back drive through the vegetable garden, across the path to the front of the house and back again. It had been a fairly wet week and in their laps of racing duly carved up a section of the Prince's wildflower border. We put it right as best as we could, and they had a fantastic weekend.

'What if the Prince comments about the restructuring of his wild flower border?' I mentioned to Diana.

'Oh, I wouldn't worry about that, Ken,' she replied. 'He's got plenty!'

The following weekend when he was there, he came out to me and said, 'I gather you had a marvellous weekend with some go-karts?'

'Yes, Sir, it was very good – William was instrumental in forming out his own Grand Prix.'

'Yes, I know,' he would say, and then with the familiar haunting grimace, would add, 'You're not thinking of becoming the next Bernie Ecclestone, are you?' He thankfully made no reference to his ploughed-up flower border.

There are so many stories from so many different outlets and more and more people are speaking of their stories. Even after so long, so many people are still fascinated. We came back from Nevis and a colleague who shall remain nameless felt unwell on the flight home. Diana was painting her nails and he was completely out of it – so far out of it that she managed to paint his nails too without him having any idea of what she was up to! She had a prankish side, she was very much a joker. He left the aircraft with both hands in his pockets, with Diana beside herself with laughter as my colleague bashfully climbed into an awaiting Range Rover.

She was always up for a risqué joke – that kept her going in a way and it was part of her character to enjoy herself. Royal life didn't give her the excitement or fun she craved but I feel that she did manage to achieve her primary aim, which was to ensure that her boys became good people, that they didn't rest on who they were because of an accident of birth. We may still have some way to go before we know exactly what path both men will take, but what we know for sure is that they were given a fantastic childhood and a fantastic model of loving, caring parenting from their mother.

CHAPTER 20

ROS COWARD

'The greatest problem in the world today is intolerance.
Everyone is so intolerant of each other.'

JUST AS THEY do with all women and all representations of womanhood, the media set up binary situations with the women in the Royal Family – the good princess and the bad princess, the beautiful princess and the ugly princess. Relatively early in Diana's marriage, there was a preoccupation with her versus Sarah Ferguson, with Fergie taking the negative roles: the 'Duchess of Pork', as the tabloids called her, against Diana, the beautiful princess. This splitting of people into binary oppositions has been played out again around Kate and Meghan, the dutiful versus the selfish, and indeed William and Harry as the good brother and the bad brother. Tabloids seem to have a need to have someone to hate, and the Royals sometimes offer particularly rich pickings.

It's not uncommon to hear commentators say that Diana manipulated the press. Diana was very media-savvy, but there is a world of difference between using the media and manipulating them. She was aware of her power, often asking, 'Why doesn't the Royal Family use me? I have all of this press following me around, I could be used,' She knew the game and how it could be played. Whether this was collusion is another question – in the time leading up to her death, there were tip-offs when she was at various places, such as on Dodi Fayed's boat in St-Tropez. There is a suggestion that, because her relationship with the heart surgeon Hasnat Khan had faltered, Diana was hoping to send a message of *Look what you're missing!* to him by being seen and photographed with Dodi. Again, this is a very relatable move, and one which many engage in at the end of a relationship.

But the accusations she was manipulative are, to a considerable extent, misogynistic and largely due to her power. Diana was extraordinarily compelling and charismatic and there seems to have been a refusal to accept that this was an attribute she had naturally, not something she concocted to gain advantages over Prince Charles. Some of the photographers I interviewed said that, with most people and celebrities, you have a roll of film and hope for one picture that can be used; with Diana there would be one picture that *couldn't* be used, the rest were all perfect. One photographer said that she had the sort of face that 'assembled' itself in front of the camera and always looked engaging and beautiful. People simply fell under her spell because of these star qualities, and because of them she was a valuable source of income to photographers. Journalist Roy Greenslade once called her 'the Princess of Sales', and that applied throughout the 1980s, when the press didn't know what had hit them and simply could not get enough of her. Here was a glamorous member of the first-tier Royal Family, wearing fashionable clothes and looking remarkable – all of their dreams had come true. She evolved before their eyes and, importantly, she interacted with them and treated them as human beings. For the press gang, she was gold dust.

Her mother Frances told me that when Diana was first engaged and was still living with a group of friends in Pimlico, the press got wind of this 'Shy Di' who was likely to become the future Princess of Wales. From then on they followed the nineteen-year-old everywhere. Frances wrote to the papers at that point, telling them to leave her daughter alone because it was impossible for anyone to cope with that level of media attention. In fact, Diana did manage the situation to some extent with her charm and her teasing; she laughed with the royal photographers and recognised them individually, which brought her a lot of good coverage. When she died, many of those same photographers were genuinely upset. Yes, they had made careers out of her, but they had also been beside her as she had changed into the woman she was to be for many years. They had documented her growth and her development until the end, when photographers, especially freelance paparazzi, became much more intrusive.

After Diana's divorce she was much more at the mercy of paparazzi, a very different type of photographer from those in the royal press pack. These freelancers would often try to elicit a reaction from Diana by calling her the most awful names. The boundaries, the respect, had been so broken down by the time the marriage disintegrated that they seemed to feel they were entitled to do that. Some of these photographers even boasted about how they got their shots – about how they stuck the camera in Diana's face and said terrible things, sometimes making her cry until she pushed them away, all of which was often presented as perfectly acceptable.

Sometimes they shouted 'bitch' and much worse at her, so that there was almost a free-for-all after she gave up her royal protection. When Ken left, she lost a level of protection that wasn't simply security-based, but human. He would often negotiate with the press, offering them one or two shots of Diana in exchange for her being left alone for the rest of a trip or holiday, and this entente cordiale proved very successful for all parties. But foreign paparazzi had their own rules – or lack of them – and often pushed the boundaries of privacy and decency well beyond those of the British media.

In this context, suggesting that Diana 'used' the press seems like a significant misrepresentation. It is more that she was canny about the value of press involvement, until it got out of hand. She understood that coverage could bring leverage for charities, and publicity that they wouldn't otherwise have received. She knew the power of publicity for her causes, such as her handshake with the AIDS patient, which was revolutionary. No other public figure had been photographed doing such a thing, which I think we forget nowadays, when there are now people who are – thankfully – living normal lives with an HIV+ diagnosis. Back then, it was seen as the 'gay plague', with almost certain death for those who were afflicted – but Diana changed so much of that with just a touch. She knew the power of an image.

Everyone I spoke to who had been involved with one of Diana's charities told of how her involvement changed everything – it was golden. It meant guaranteed publicity for events or causes. When she was linked to Great Ormond Street very early on in her royal 'career', the hospital hit its funding targets almost as soon as the campaign opened. All of these groups were sympathetic to what she had to put up with, but they knew that, without it, their own aims and objectives would never have been reached. She was an asset, and people knew that.

Some photographers told me that they would never have dared miss an event where Diana was out and about. Usually, when they followed Royals, the event would be deadly boring and they would get off home as soon as they could, with dull shots of dull people. With Diana, there was usually something spontaneous and thrilling. She knew how to make events special, even the rather dreary ones. She had a reputation for making them all significant to the charity workers and the public who turned up and there were always images to record such interactions. She could make everyone feel like the most important person in the room. The media found her incredibly engaging and addictive because there was often a shot of Diana kneeling down to talk to a child, or tenderly touching someone's face, or putting her arm around someone to offer sympathy. In Bosnia she asked the driver to stop the car she was travelling in when she spotted a woman in a cemetery. Although they had no shared language, Diana put her arm around her and the woman, who had lost her son in the Bosnian War, wept on her shoulder. The press knew that there would always be moments like this.

There is no doubt that Diana and the media had a symbiotic relationship, with both parties getting something out of it. It's all too easy to label any such interaction as manipulative when a woman is involved, to say that she was wrapping them around her finger, but she paid the price on many occasions – especially, of course, ultimately. These accusations are typical of the misogyny which was levelled at Diana. Allegations that she was 'mentally unstable' often levelled at her by the 'B' team – certain courtiers and friends of Charles – labelled her in a way that women have faced from the dawn of time. That again encapsulated how Diana could be seen as 'everywoman'. Her status didn't protect her from these insults, from these undermining comments that are thrown at any woman who steps out of line. Nicolas Soames, after the Bashir interview, said that Diana was in the 'advanced stages of paranoia'. To be called 'crazy' is one of the standard retorts to any woman who questions what's happening, and being royalty doesn't get you a free pass.

The Andrew Morton book and the Martin Bashir interview were Diana's opportunity to get her views across, but they were achieved in quite an amateurish way, whether it was James Colthurst dropping off taped recordings to Morton, or Bashir being smuggled into Kensington Palace. Neither book nor interview could be called a professionally waged campaign, but both threatened the Establishment enough that Diana was attacked as a result. It was shocking to many members of the establishment that she poured out her heart, but their reaction was predictable. Many of them saw her actions as disloyal and, due to their lack of understanding of mental health issues, they weren't particularly sympathetic. Her stress and anxiety were dismissed.

Now, with all of the information coming out about what Bashir did in order to secure the interview, it's very clear that Diana was the one being manipulated and that the so-called manipulative moments had huge consequences for her own life. There was no turning back after the Bashir interview. But Diana did get her voice out there.

During her participation in the Morton book, Diana, it seems, was still hoping that the marriage could be saved, although at the same time she clearly felt very despondent about what had happened. But if Charles had said, 'Let's see what we can do – let's try to fix this,' she probably would have willingly tried, not least because she wanted to shield her boys from the experience of parental divorce. On numerous occasions, interviewees for my book insisted she had never wanted to divorce and had, at least until much later on, hoped that something could be resolved. Even with her knowledge of what was going betwen Charles and Camilla, her focus was still on trying to make her marriage better. People can hold two conflicting hopes – it's perfectly understandable that Diana could have still wanted it to work, while nursing anger about the situation she had been put in with Camilla. A lot of her behaviour was probably retaliatory. Her affair with James Hewitt undoubtedly brought her some pleasure – he behaved quite well towards her, and he gave her comfort – but Diana's priority was for the marriage to work, and it seems likely that she had affairs because she was lonely. A lot of her behaviours and reactions were actually very normal when we look at it that way – she was lonely, she was isolated, she was being told these things weren't happening when, actually, people were colluding in Charles and Camilla's affair. Why wouldn't she act the way she did?

The press's relationship with Diana was nothing if not complicated, so it's hardly surprising that she did not control the agenda and sometimes misjudged how her actions would be received. There was a lot of scathing commentary around her in the last year of her life. Even when she did amazing things, such as her Angola and Bosnia trips, there was plenty of negative coverage – in fact, in her last few weeks, there was a great deal of pretty nasty comments, all of which was forgotten after the fatal crash, when 'other' media outlets could be blamed.

In 1996, Diana had watched a heart operation being performed at Harefield Hospital by Professor Sir Magdi Yacoub. The patient was a little boy from Cameroon who had been brought to England by Chain of Hope, a charity Diana supported. She was much criticised for wearing heavy eye make-up during the surgery and for looking directly at a press photographer on a number of occasions from above her face mask.

Diana did try to keep some aspects of her life entirely away from press coverage. Details of her relationship with Hasnat Khan, also a heart surgeon, through her ongoing interest in heart charities, was kept below the radar. She was genuinely keen on him – he seemed to be very straightforward, not a glitzy man, not in the mould of Dodi Fayed, but a man who was wrapped up in his work. In Khan she had fallen for a quiet, serious person, someone who wanted no attention for himself. But that was the death knell for their love. It seems that Khan was the one who ended it because he couldn't bear the public nature of life with Diana – there didn't seem to be any future with the world's most famous woman. He wasn't that sort of person at all and had no wish to be involved in any kind of media attention. Since then, Khan has respected her privacy about whatever happened between them, which seems entirely in keeping with the character he displayed at that time.

Did Diana think she could simply turn into someone who would marry a heart surgeon and slide into middle-class obscurity, perhaps with another child? She probably did have a fantasy of that kind, but it would never have happened. She did make a sad comment along the lines of, *Who would ever take me on, who would want me?* The differences between Hasnat Khan and Dodi Fayed make those words even more poignant. Maybe she thought Dodi could have coped better with all of that, but it seems likely this wasn't a desperately serious liaison. Given that the relationship with Khan ended very close to the summer holiday with Dodi – probably just about six weeks before she died. – it would be rather soon for her then to be in another meaningful affair. She and Dodi may very well have been attracted to each other, and he knew the world of glitz and grandeur, but was it a deep connection? It's unlikely.

Diana's relationship with the media ended with a pack of photographers chasing her through a road tunnel in Paris. Even as she lay dying, they poked cameras at the car windows. In spite of the public abhorrence at this, Diana's death has not led to as much change in the media's relationship with the Royal Family as initially seemed likely. There was the huge outpouring of grief when she died, with blame focusing on the foreign paparazzi. But even the more 'respectable' media were subject to criticism for how eagerly they had exploited the image of Diana, and how readily they ran intrusive stories about her private life. In the aftermath of her death, the immediate détente was that the British press agreed not to stalk William and Harry while they were children, and to some extent they stuck by that. The boys did have an adolescence relatively free of press intrusion – apart from a few incidents of Harry drinking and smoking dope. It wasn't until they were in their early adulthood that the press began to return to their old ways: front pages of Harry at a fancy-dress party in a Nazi outfit, Harry in Vegas in a hot tub. The legacy was, for them, that they were given a much gentler ride than might have happened had Diana still been alive. It's quite easy to imagine there would have been more intrusion, and a sense that the three of them would have been acceptable prey.

It has become very clear from the treatment of Meghan that many of the media's old ways are still there, and that she pays the price for being an independent woman with her own mind, one who won't simply accept royal life because that's how things have always been in that world. Like Diana, Meghan became someone whose every public interaction was scrutinised, and the intolerance the former often experienced has certainly shown itself rather cruelly in much of the coverage of her daughter-in-law.

In the last interview she gave before she died, Diana spoke of having a public profile and a public position allowing her to do things. That comes across as an overwhelming priority for her – the trips to Angola and Bosnia seem to have been very energising for her and placed her on a global platform where she felt she had found a way to use her celebrity for international causes. That indication that she still wanted to be on the world stage doesn't fit with any notion of being the wife of a committed heart surgeon who wanted no publicity, but Diana was never straightforward.

There is no single portrait of Diana's life which gives this whole story, so it is unsurprising, in a way, that press coverage never seemed to get it exactly right. In many ways she seemed rather lost and lonely towards the end of her life. Yet at the same time she was also clearly quite fulfilled with her charity involvement and her campaigning. She also looked comfortable in her own skin, appearing powerful, strong and charismatic in her final photos.

Diana was someone who had the capacity to be happy and funny, which sometimes makes people think she was a fake given that we knew so much of her misery. But that appears to have been her gift: she could find the joy in things even when other aspects were quite desperate. She was multi-faceted and perhaps that was what we found so unusual, for we simply hadn't seen a fully rounded member of the Royal Family before.

CHAPTER 21

KEN WHARFE

'The biggest disease the world suffers from,
in this day and age, is the disease of people
feeling unloved.'

WHEN I FIRST went to Kensington Palace in the mid-1980s,
I didn't really recognise any sort of media involvement at
all. One thing which struck me was how friendly Diana was with the
media, and that was just the characteristic she had, a very outgoing
personality that almost encouraged her to speak to anybody. She
understood the media and saw the importance of them getting
the right story. At that point, about 90 per cent of the coverage
towards her, maybe more, was very positive and she had no axe to
grind about any stories, Interestingly enough, I remember Diana
saying a few words to William on his first day at school in 1987 as
a five-year-old:

'Look, I want you to behave yourself so when you get to school
there will be a lot of photographers there. You need to learn to
behave yourself because this will happen to you for the rest of your
life.' Those were profound words – although somewhat punctured

by William frowning at her from below his school cap and declaring, 'I know but I don't like 'tographers!' I thought then, *Why are you saying you don't like them when you have no real experience of them?* It dawned on me later that he said that because, every morning without fail, the red top newspapers would be laid out for Diana on top of the chest freezer in the kitchen. Diana would routinely go down to the kitchen to have a bowl of cereal beside the chefs and glance at the newspapers. William and Harry would inevitably turn up from their breakfast in the nursery, and occasionally the older Prince would see things he didn't like that had been printed. That can be his only reason for saying he didn't like ''tographers' at such a young age.

Diana was very aware of what people were saying about her – like any of us, if people say nice things, we buy it, and the Royal Family are no different. Many assumptions are made that the Queen and the rest of them don't read what is said – but I can assure you that they do, they all get a daily press coverage given to them, so they're very much aware of the news in relation to them.

The Princess of Wales was very aware of the power of the media but, at this point, very little was being said that was derogatory. As time went on, and as the Camilla issue was given more daylight, I feel things really unravelled, in that it was often sidelined by those in the 'B team' as Diana's paranoia. But she was right – it was a problem. She rode the storm at that point, up until the 1992 Andrew Morton book. But she had told me in the mid-1980s in Spain about Camilla and about James Hewitt. That she had told me so quickly and so openly showed how much it mattered to her and how it important it was for her to get her situation over to anyone who would be working in such close quarters with her.

She knew what was going on, her friends knew what was going on, but the outside world thought she was paranoid about a relationship that didn't exist – but she was right, it *did* exist. This was such a frustration for her, and she was trying to find a way to put things in its true perspective.

The press knew very well what was going on between Charles and Camilla, but there was a reluctance to print it in any great detail because of the uncertainty of what might result if they did. The Prince had his own press office which was very powerful – Diana merely shared the same facility, she didn't command the loyalty which was directed at her husband by his staff there. Even when she acquired her own press officer much later, the man who held the position – Dickie Arbiter – bestrode both camps, for he was also the Prince of Wales's press secretary. I guess it must have been difficult for him as he would know of the existence of Camilla, but as a true press officer he had to be diplomatic in how he released information. Before Morton, I saw the pressure building and Diana getting anxious. Later, when the Prince worked with Jonathan Dimbleby on a book, it was Richard Aylard, his private secretary, who reportedly persuaded him to give a TV interview about it all with Dimbleby. As I understand it, Charles wasn't keen as he was fearful about the Camilla issue being raised but, let's be honest, that was what people wanted to hear about. They weren't terribly interested in hearing about the plants at Highgrove or the ancient trees surrounding the estate.

There was an embarrassing moment in the interview when Dimbleby asked Charles when he had started seeing Camilla again, and the Prince replied, with his usual grimace, 'When the relationship had irretrievably broken down.' Of course that wasn't necessarily accurate, and people knew it. His response completely inflamed Diana and no doubt added to her wish to go public with the Bashir interview. Although we now know that she was manipulated into that with false claims and false 'supporting' documents, it doesn't detract from the fact that she was right about Camilla and she wanted to be heard.

Diana had actually been to the Queen and told her of the issues between them and was told in no uncertain way, 'It's not my problem – it's up to you to speak to your husband, it's not for me to speak to my son.'

And that was the dilemma for Diana. 'I can never speak to him about it! He denies it all – what can I do?' This situation was no different to any other marital breakdown in which there is a third party involved, but what made this complicated was that this was a Royal marriage and it was all being played out in the national media. She was right – there were three of them in that marriage from beginning to end, and I'm not actually sure how it sustained itself for as long as it did. It was the 40th birthday party for Annabel Elliot, Camilla's sister, which was the last straw for Diana, where she thought, *There's no point in me trying to keep this thing alive.*

I find the Morton incident very interesting. James Colthurst was the go-between, a friend of Diana's who she had known since they were both teenagers. He was the one who delivered the tapes to Morton once Diana had recorded her story onto them – he did so rather incongruously in his pink cashmere sweater, on his old lady bicycle with a wicker basket on front, a basket containing those damning tapes. He has since said that he often feared for his life, had his task been uncovered. Although the book wasn't penned by Diana, it was effectively her memoir – Morton basically transcribed her words. He was actually a relatively junior journalist at that time who had met Colthurst over a game of squash and hatched the whole business. Diana very happily released that information through Colthurst and no one knew about it – I was working with her at the time, and I had no idea.

It was one of the very few things she had never confided in me – but if she had, I would probably have said it was a crazy idea. The negative outcome wasn't actually as bad as I thought it would be; it came and it went remarkably quickly.

Her brother-in-law, Robert Fellowes, who was married to her elder sister, and who was a private secretary to the Queen, was angry about it, and asked her, 'When did you speak to Morton about all this?'

'I've never spoken to him,' Diana replied.

No one could believe that, but it was completely true – it was all through tapes and a third party. Diana had achieved, after many years, exactly what she wanted – and that was to tell the truth about her relationship, the truth about her marriage. There was no other way to do it; she had to get the facts out there in her own words as they would be tampered with or dismissed if she went down any other route.

When I asked her about the secrecy of it all after discovering what she had done, Diana had clearly thought it all out:

'You and everybody else would have advised me not to do it, Ken, and that would have placed more pressure on me. I only wanted the pressure to come from me. It was a decision that I made, and I made it because I wanted to do it.'

With hindsight, it has become a reference book to the life of Diana because of the facts she revealed. It was a factual account of the true, short-lived life of a princess of the British monarchy. You can't improve on that. History tends to rely on what courtiers say or books by third parties. Before I first put pen to paper, there had been eighty-two books already written about Diana and only the one by Paul Burrell had actually been written by someone who knew her. Historically, then, we have an intriguing document with that Morton book and everything she said in it was true.

She had been very open and even innocent with many of her interactions up to that point, and the fact that she was able to keep this enormous secret and execute it perfectly was the evolution of a new Diana; it almost showed what the Royal Family had done to her, they had changed her character. I wasn't hurt that she hadn't told me, but I was surprised. I understood why she'd done it and that was fine, she'd made her own decision and she was perfectly at liberty to do that. She liaised with Morton directly, and once I read the book, I knew she had spoken the truth – is it not right that we should have it? It's far better to have it all in her own words than through a series of people who never knew her.

Up until the mid-1980s when I arrived, Diana was the servant of the Queen – her role was to represent the Queen, looking wonderful, opening up leisure centres and doing what the monarch expected her to do. She had ticked all of those boxes and was desperate to do something else. The chance of a reconciliation with Charles was fading by the day and I think there had been a sea change when she realised she wanted to forge her own path, both in terms of the causes she supported and also for herself. She would still help out, she would still do joint engagements, but those things were a problem for Charles, not her. There is no doubt that he was jealous of the love and affection felt for Diana by the public and, as someone who was desperate to be seen as a serious, intelligent future monarch, her popularity was the issue for him – and for the rest of the Royal Family. They couldn't harness her popularity for their own good, and they didn't even try – however, it was something she owned.

On Charles and Diana's first joint engagement abroad in Australia with William, such was the crowd pull of Diana that it left the Prince almost stranded. There was an extraordinary speech he gave on the second day, in Sydney, when he said, 'I'm very pleased to be here – the next time I come, I'll bring two wives. I'll put one on either side of the road and just walk down the middle.' We all laughed but that was a serious point – he was unhappy with what he was witnessing. I saw it so many times.

After Morton, newspapers wanted to dig even deeper and find out even more about this remarkable Royal marriage and Diana felt she had nothing to lose. What would be wrong with speaking to journalists such as Richard Kay? She had no support – why not do whatever she pleased?

The summer after the Morton book, she had met a senior executive at Disney, Sid Bass, who had said, 'Come over, come to Orlando, I'll set it all up. You'll have a great time.'

I went over to recce the trip and spoke to the entire Disney board in Florida, who made available virtually everything you could think of to make her stay perfect. Diana had assured me that she hadn't spoken to anyone about it, but I needed to make sure that was the case. However, I had this hunch that someone already knew we were going – I asked the security there to check the accommodation lists and, lo and behold, I found a Richard Kay booked in. His presence didn't alarm me, but it did flag up that Diana had been talking to him in the knowledge that he would always write very positive pieces and he was a good contact for her. I later discovered, when I left, that she had many more – I guess that was to have some equilibrium, given that the Prince had so many contacts.

Disneyworld was a great experience for them. A lady called Jane Keir looked after us there and set up an extraordinary holiday for them. I once went with Diana and the boys on a float boat across a small manmade lake to an island for a mid-western style 'hoop-de-do'. We sat at a table among hundreds of other families. There was an old 'joanna' on the stage, and staff dressed up as cowboys with lassos. The pianist caught the eye of William and shouted over, 'Hey buddy! Come over and do the hoop-de-do!'

William was dead keen to get on stage, followed by Harry. Everyone had hats on and were dancing, and they had terrific fun. There was no press, the press couldn't get to us there – at the end, we got back on our float boat to the Grand Floridian hotel. Diana was beside herself with happiness, as were the boys.

'God, that was a real night, wasn't it, Ken?' she said to me. 'I never thought I'd do anything like that with my kids, them performing on stage with not one single photographer there.' It would have been a press delight to see these two young Princes do that, but we got away with it.

Elsewhere at Disneyworld, I had to eventually drag Harry off Space Mountain. I became rather dizzy we'd been on so often – because of who the boys were, they had the option to just get off a ride and go straight back on. There is an underground network at Disneyworld which is a replica of what is on the surface. The cast members and maintenance staff access the site that way; instead of queueing at the front, we used that option too and came out at the rides from underneath. The press didn't like that as they would try and guess where Diana and the boys were going to be, but they popped up from a hole underneath the park to walk straight onto a ride.

We were helped by a guy called Dave Benson, a US state department official who looked like someone straight out of central casting. I'd met Dave when I did the first reconnaissance and when we arrived, Diana fell in love with him. He was a big guy, 6 feet 4 inches, a typical American, completely at one with her. He was her best mate instantly, as he was with everyone. 'You're looking great, Ma'am, you're looking fantastic,' he would tell her casually. Diana had a six-room suite in the Grand Floridian hotel and the entire floor covering was Snow White tufted carpet, as if four inches of snow had fallen.

One day, Diana said to me, 'Oh, Ken, where's your friend Dave?'

'I'll call him up,' I replied.

'I'm downstairs, having a quick burger,' Dave told me, 'but I can come up and see her. Not a problem.'

He was still munching into his massive great burger when he arrived.

'Come in, Dave,' said Diana, delighted to see him.

'Sorry about the burger, Ma'am,' he apologised. With that, a huge blob of ketchup jettisoned out of the burger and dropped onto the snowy white carpet. We all started laughing and Diana thought nothing of it, while Dave apologised profusely.

'I'm so sorry, Ma'am – I just need to make a call,' which he did. 'We have a problem in the suite – send a man up with a carpet cleaner.' Almost instantly, this guy appeared with a wooden box, a roll of carpet, a pot of glue and a Stanley knife. He cut out this piece of stained carpet, put in another of the same size, glued it in, and gave a cheery goodbye as he left. 'Have a magical day!' he said. Diana thought this was one of the most entertaining things she'd seen.

'Thank you, Dave,' she said.

'Not a problem – we do these things all the time.' I'm sure he didn't have tomato ketchup-stained white carpet replaced in a matter of minutes for British Princesses at Disneyworld, but he seemed completely nonplussed.

Those were good times for Diana, but it wouldn't be long until she would be facing the fallout from her revelations, which was totally negative. I knew what had happened and I knew her, and so, watching it, there was nothing new for me. I didn't really have a problem with it because I thought at the time, what choice did she have? In 1995, she was effectively no longer a member of the Royal Family, so if this was what she really wanted to do, could we blame her? People didn't like it – particularly the establishment as they were very much against airing your dirty laundry in public. These were changing times and Diana was now very much a loose cannon – but an accurate one. Had she peddled mistruths and fake news, that would have been a different story. From my own observations, there wasn't one single line in that interview which was incorrect. Historically, it's gone down as one of the most intriguing interviews of all time, never mind one that featured a Royal talking about her marital problems with a man who was in line to be King.

It was a bombshell for Diana to say she felt that Charles wasn't suitable to become King, but I do believe it was something she firmly believed. It's arguable that, for the thirteen years she was a working member of the Royal Family, she knew him very well.

She didn't see him much towards the end when things were very difficult between them but, more so than anyone, she was entitled to that opinion. There are those who would disagree, notably the establishment who would support him, but she was right to voice her opinion.

The Morton book was important to Diana, but the Bashir interview meant more – when her brother told her of the 'evidence' Bashir brought, she would have thought, *I'm not wrong here – I've always felt that people are spying on me and now there is proof.* It makes sense that she was behaving so differently in 1993 as she was starting to believe everyone around her was a spy, working for the establishment to, in her words, 'make her go away'. I only found out about the Bashir interview when the rest of the world did. How she kept it all as tight as she did was remarkable.

In the early 2020s, the Dyson Report then proved that Bashir secured that interview through a series of lies, which is one reason why the story still rumbles on. Initially, the idea that a BBC interview had secured an interview with Diana was a huge coup. I don't think she could have trusted Paul Burrell at that point; he was laid off that night – he was too risky a subject to be allowed in. She would have known that. She was becoming suspicious of Burrell anyway. Towards the end, he too was being seen as a troubling presence and he knew that as he was seeking vacancies abroad at that time.

Diana is still having an impact on the public discourse around the Royal Family and perhaps she has slightly changed the way some of the other members engage with the public, but none of it has anywhere near the impact she had. One of the things she did when she put people at their ease was talk about things they were interested in, rather than a world they had no knowledge or experience of. She had no time for establishment small talk. She would rather be with someone on the street than a lord lieutenant. That was what made her happy and what still endears her to the public. The Americans have a vision of royalty being so far removed in castles with drawbridges and moats, but they could see Diana was a modern princess who came out of that world and did things no one had ever done before.

Queen Victoria was actually the first to ever go out from the front of Buckingham Palace to ride in an open carriage up Constitution Hill and back again – in doing so, she was subjected to seven assassination attempts, which may have made the monarchy somewhat wary of public interaction! Along came Diana many years later and opened up the relationship between royalty and the public in a very different way. She broke the mould and that is why we still talk about her. Added to that, the vast majority of people feel she was duped by the Prince of Wales. There is no doubt she changed the face of the monarchy, but where would that have gone? Who knows? She was a campaigner for widening the access of the Royal Family to people and she was a campaigner for so much more; that would no doubt have continued.

The Palace knew what they had in Diana, but they didn't want to acknowledge it. The turning point was when she had that conversation with the Queen about AIDS. They had been prepared to let it run but that was a sea change. Diana would say to me many times, 'I do this because I enjoy it – it's my job. I have no qualifications, I'm not well educated but at least I'm doing something I'm good at. It would be great if someone in the family could acknowledge that.'

It never happened. They knew her work with AIDS sufferers would bring even more attention, and when the Queen told her to deal with something 'nice', she saw what they really thought. The Royal Family absolutely hated it. It catapulted her to even greater, positive public awareness. It stole their thunder and their purpose. The closest Diana ever got to a public acknowledgement was when the Queen commented after her death. She knew what she was doing – she knew that by taking on this subject she would provoke controversy within her own camp, and she was spot on.

I remember going with her to launch a nuclear submarine in Barrow-in-Furness, where there was a major policing problem. There were cries then of why she was getting involved in such a thing. Initially the Prince was to do it, but when he pulled out, I did the reconnaissance in conjunction with the Ministry of Defence. We knew that by launching this first of four nuclear submarines, there would be political demonstrations, notably from the camps in Faslane. We agreed that we would helicopter into the shipyard and helicopter back out again. It was only when descending in the helicopter that I got railroaded by the Chief Constable, who said there were thousands of people in the town of Barrow who knew Diana was there.

'I've never seen so many people in these streets in my entire working life,' he told me. 'There is no way we can't give these people something of this woman they've been desperate to see for weeks.'

I was adamant. 'No, I can't approve that. I can't allow it. The risk of a demonstration is too great.'

'What's going on, Ken? I don't mind doing it. I'll go and wave a few flags,' said Diana.

In the end, I was overruled. Instead of staying in the shipyard confines, we did a left turn and there were thousands of flag-waving people – lovely until we got back to the shipyard and we found ourselves in a dead end. The one thing you never do is stop at a dead end – you need to be able to go somewhere or be able to turn back round. We stopped and 20 or 30 demonstrators dressed as the Ku Klux Klan came over the barriers and slammed on the car before eventually being arrested. It should never have happened – six months of security assessments had been overruled simply to appease the Barrow public. I understood they wanted to see her, but it was too big a risk. Why had the Prince of Wales been pulled out of that engagement? Once it had been changed to Diana, the world and his dog turned up. They weren't interested in anything but her.

If Diana's relationship with James Hewitt had worked and a divorce was possible at that time, she would have taken a low-key life out of the public eye if possible, away from the life she was already living, but that would have been almost impossible. She didn't really have that many relationships, they were very short-lived as it was virtually impossible to sustain one in that }environment, particularly a sexual relationship. The opportunities for that were so few.

I think she did see a chance for some normal life with Hasnat Khan – but by then she was a global icon and it couldn't happen. Who knows what more time could have given her? Khan saw the problem, as did his relatives in Pakistan, who swam for the shore dramatically and just could not take the relationship. She was the consummate performer on the stage while working as a princess but she never really wanted it to be for the rest of her life – finding a way out of that was very hard. Khan was probably her best hope of a normal life. He was single, he had a profession and she saw the possibility of that working, whether here or in Pakistan. I think she underestimated her own popularity and thought, *I'm out of that family now I'm no longer an HRH, I'm free to do what I want so what's the problem?* She failed to realise that she was still a draw. The press attention wasn't as electric as it had been but anything untoward, especially with Khan, was magnetic news to the world's media.

As she witnessed herself with Dodi in the months leading up to her death, the media still wanted to see what she was doing. That relationship, I believe, could well have been a statement of resentment, of protest against what had happened with Khan. Any man who turned up on the scene was immediately deemed to be a lover, and I had that levelled at me too! I sued many newspapers, including the *Guardian*, who said Diana was buying me shirts! They settled immediately, as did the others, as they knew they had no evidence. I may have been someone who had seen a Diana that very few knew even existed, but there was certainly never anything like that between us.

CHAPTER 22

ROS COWARD

*'I'd like to be a queen of people's hearts ... but I don't
see myself being the queen of this country.'*

THE NATIONAL OUTPOURING of grief after Diana's death was astonishing: people were walking about in the streets, distressed, crying, laying flowers outside Kensington and Buckingham Palaces, unable to comprehend what had happened. Ordinary life seemed to have come to a stop, and for a time there was an almost feverish atmosphere. One of the things that started happening was that amounts of money in envelopes arrived at Kensington Palace – a pound with a little note from a child, another pound from an OAP. Suddenly, money started pouring in, with £25 million (equivalent to about £43 million today) appearing from public donations from people who wanted to make a contribution to the charitable world of Diana. In retrospect it shows just how far she touched ordinary people, people who felt moved to send in small amounts of money that added up to a great deal, especially when placed alongside the royalties from Elton John's version of 'Candle in the Wind', adapted in memory of Diana.

Questions about how to handle the money and where it should go resulted in the fairly hasty creation of the Diana, Princess of Wales Memorial Fund. Staff from Kensington Palace, including Paul Burrell, Diana's former part-time private secretary Michael Gibbins and a few people who had been working in the back offices, were hastily drawn in to deal with it. Also the representatives of Diana's estate were involved from the beginning. This estate had been established after her death and would look after her property. Its trustees included her mother, Frances Shand Kydd, her sister Sarah McCorquodale, and the Bishop of London. They were concerned with guarding the long-term interests (including proprietorial interests) of Diana and her memory, which is how the Memorial Fund came to be involved in controlling the use of her name and identity. Also among the trustees recruited to the fund were people who were experienced in the world of charities and voluntary organisations. It seems there was a tension from the beginning between some of those who came from Kensington Palace, who had little experience of administering such an enterprise, and those who came from the more professional world of charities. Paul Burrell was part of the Kensington Palace group and very much saw his role as keeping the Diana flame burning. He went to events, gave interviews, and generally contributed to a highly emotional remembrance of her wherever he could. The more professional side was concerned more with carving out a distinctive pathway for the fund, trying to work out what sort of charity it should be. It defined itself as being a grant-giving charity which would give money to some of the distinctive causes with which Diana had been involved, such as landmines, AIDS, and hospices.

I have been told that from the beginning Diana's estate may have anticipated that the Royal Family wouldn't necessarily want the fund to be a permanent body, and so acted accordingly. As a result, the fund slowly defined itself as a body that would eventually disburse all the money it raised to charities with which Diana had been involved or would have supported. At first look this is surprising given how much money poured in and the probable assumptions made by those contributing that it would be a permanent memorial to her, but perhaps less so given the reservations which both the Royals and Diana's estate seem to have had about the Memorial Fund being permanent, keeping memories of Diana for ever in people's minds.

The fund also raised money from licensing various products connected with Diana's name and identity. The use of her name on tubs of Flora margarine ended rather disastrously. Paul Burrell and Sarah McCorquodale were key in setting up the deal with Flora. Burrell, in particular, saw it as a happy use of her name – he ran the London Marathon to promote the Flora initiative and raise money for the fund. It did indeed generate quite a lot of funds, but there was also a great deal of criticism that the move was tacky. This led to some public scepticism about what the trustees of the fund were doing and how they were allowing Diana's image to be used: a signature on a margarine tub didn't quite fit in with the ostensible control of Diana's name to reflect her dignity.

There was a great deal of money coming in, and with it the potential to make much more from commercial deals, but while the fund gave the go-ahead to Flora margarine, other collaborations and attempts to use Diana's name and image were not supported. One of the attempts to control her image went badly, resulting in a legal dispute with the famous Franklin Mint in Pennsylvania. Among coins, medals and other collectibles, the company makes 'heirloom' porcelain dolls of notable people, so it is not at all surprising that they decided to produce a Diana doll. However, the Memorial Fund tried to stop it by legal action, as they saw it as 'tacky'. Franklin Mint won the court case and it cost the fund dearly. Franklin Mint then countersued for defamation against being called 'tacky' and grasping, when it was a reputable company. The case was eventually settled out of court, but the whole saga cost the fund about £12 million, or more according to some estimates. This was a blow not only to the fund but to the trustees, who were largely serious people trying to develop a distinctive charity that would have contributed to various organisations which had difficulty getting funding elsewhere, and which were in the character of Diana's humanitarian interests. Instead, they had to spend time and money on an ill-fated and ultimately costly lawsuit.

The licensing of Diana's name did make a lot of money for the fund, but it was never a simple process. What some saw as 'tasteful', others saw as tacky. There had, for instance, been talk at one point to link up with the campaign against blood diamonds and perhaps sell ethical jewellery with guaranteed provenance, but this was seen by the estate as too personal and ill-guided. The whole commercial area was difficult and there was an internalised reluctance to actively do something positive with it to ensure a continual memory.

Paul Burrell's connection with the fund also created tensions. He threw himself into his role there and initially did some good. He was very keen to make personal appearances and give talks, enjoying the publicity. He felt that the conventional way of memorialising someone was not what Diana's memory needed, and that the fund should be more like her in its way of operating. The charity suggested that he should have found his role in a specific fundraising way rather than influencing the deals being set up. This I interpret as meaning that they wanted him to be more in line with the general direction of the organisation, and they were on the point of moving him aside when he stormed off. He gave some very scathing interviews about the Memorial Fund, saying that it was failing to keep the true spirit of Diana alive and that he was the only one who knew how to do that. After that, there was no way he could stay.

There were so many other tensions running through it all. One of the questions history might ask would be why William and Harry were so little involved in the charity – it's said that both the estate and the Royal Family wanted for there to be no pressure put on them at all about being identified as part of the charity or being figureheads, which was actually fair enough considering they were very young. People were concerned they might be wheeled out without having their own formed views about something, and subsequently might be manipulated into supporting causes they knew little about. Apparently feelings were strong about this among certain groups. On their part, it was taboo that any suggestion would be made that William and Harry would be involved in any way, shape or form. It was not exactly that a ring of steel surrounded the young princes, but it was very much the case that they should not be troubled by matters concerning the fund.

The Memorial Fund did do a lot of good and it made numerous charitable grants, charting a fairly radical pathway which was actually very much in keeping with Diana's memory. But for many people coming to the story of Diana now, it seems odd that the fund ran itself down and was eventually closed in December 2012. It is understandable that Diana's estate and Royal Family should not want to involve the princes because of worries about manipulating them. But did the Royal Family, and especially Charles, exert an unspoken influence, represented through Diana's estate, in running the fund down and letting it disappear? There doesn't seem to have been pressure applied directly, but there was an understanding, represented by the estate, about what the Royal Family wanted and that they didn't want the fund to be the focus of ongoing memory and mourning. There was never any commitment from the Royals about seeing it as a good way of remembering Diana, given that the public had poured so much money into it at the beginning.

The same questions arise about the lack of other permanent public memorials to Diana. There was an exceptional amount of difficulty when it came to any decision about a statue to memorialise Diana and it took until 2021 before it was erected, by which time Harry and William were barely speaking to each other. When you look back over history, there are many pubs, for example, that bear names of dukes and duchesses, and statues go up to all sorts of people. Yet it has been endlessly difficult to find something permanent to remember this woman who had been so adored by the public. Was there a reluctance on the part of the Royal Family to give real support to any memorialising?

It was eventually decided to run the fund down, disburse all the remaining money and cease trying to generate any more; none of the potential commercial deals that were aiming to use her name and identity were followed up. Any money left was to be given to the Royal Foundation, which was originally the joint charity of

William and Harry, and so the funds went directly there. However, the money is now divided between the two princes' charities because the Royal Foundation is now the charity of William and Kate, Harry and Meghan having left it in 2019 to pursue their own projects independently. As a result, it's extremely difficult to find out exactly how money from the original fund is distributed.

The lack of a public focus of memory for Diana is all the more shocking when you consider just what an enormous impression she made on the people she met and how overwhelming was the effect of her death. When I wrote the official book about Diana, I conducted many personal interviews with the family, who cooperated willingly because it had the backing of the Memorial Fund. Other interviews were with people who had been involved with her humanitarian work or her charities. I was very moved by a number of the interviews because even though the book was published in 2004, people did still get upset about her death, recalling how amazing she had been to them. For example, she was intensely involved with the English National Ballet; not only was she their Patron, but she went regularly to watch rehearsals and got to know people there. I spoke with Derek Deane, a former principal dancer who was Artistic Director for a while when Diana was involved, and it was clear that there was a real intensity to her connection with the ballet company. She had done an enormous amount on a personal level.

I also encountered a considerable number of ordinary people – such as people she had met in hospital, where their children were dying – with whom Diana had kept in touch and written to, and even invited them to Kensington Palace. I remember going to Northolt to see a family who had lost their child and Diana had kept in touch with them throughout and afterwards. The mother had watched as Diana's coffin arrived back at RAF Northolt from Paris and was taken through the streets. The intensity of people's feelings was strong.

Diana's death in such a brutal and unexpected accident reminded people of the arbitrariness of life, that it can be snatched away at any point and that no one is immune. People simply couldn't believe it, that Diana was dead and, for many, it brought back their own experiences of loss and sadness. While her death did not necessarily touch everyone, it was a hugely significant cultural moment. I don't recall in my lifetime any other death that has affected people in the same way, which has brought them out onto the streets: people's bewilderment at what had happened; the unbelievable ocean of flowers outside Kensington Palace; people wandering around in the vicinity. I can't think of any other death of a public figure that has had that impact apart from the effect on the American people in 1963 when they heard that JFK died.

For some, perhaps those same people who don't see the need for memorials of Diana, this grief was seen, and has been described as excessive, weird even, since the vast majority of the people mourning did not know her personally. There was a lot of commentary after the Soham murders of two young girls in 2002 which almost implied that the public expressions of grief, the flowers and the teddy bears and the football shirts, were virtually the fault of Diana – she had somehow whipped up mass hysteria from beyond the grave. In fact, Britain was already moving in this way. In 1996, the Dunblane massacre of sixteen schoolchildren and their teacher did release something in public grief and there was an outpouring of emotion at that point, too. Diana had been so in touch with the public and yet, in death, she was in many ways blamed for the manifestations of grief which were viewed in some quarters as not seemly or even not British. She had touched the people in life and she touched them in death, and both had been frowned upon by the Establishment.

Anyone who knows anything about grief and how things can be triggered knows that it is not a phoney emotion; it's what people are feeling at the time. The national paroxysm of grief in reaction to Diana's death had triggered deep feelings in many people: about an untimely death; about the tragedy of her now motherless boys; about a short life full of aspirations and frustrations; about what good can be done by one lonely person – and indeed about guilt for our own involvement in watching Diana's life so intrusively. The reaction to Diana's death didn't come as a bolt from the blue. It came from a more emotionally in-touch country, and that seems entirely appropriate – after all, that was what she was about, being in touch with our feelings. Perhaps her death really did show that she had achieved what she wanted – she had become the queen of people's hearts.

CHAPTER 23

KEN WHARFE

*'A mother's arms are more comforting
than anyone else's.'*

HARRY'S COMMENTS IN April 2022 that he is the one 'protecting' the Queen were, of course, not literal. We have to bear in mind that he's an odd mix – he was pleased that he made the journey to see his grandmother en route to Holland for the Invictus Games and, from my point of view, would very much like to be back on the scene. It would have been quite wrong to travel and yet not see her in her Jubilee Year. I think it was predictable and probably would have come up during discussions, but as to how he is protecting her, I believe that would be more in the sense of a grandson's duty. Perhaps he sees himself as a link between the generations, but it was a comment which certainly threw a lot of Royal watchers. Harry is not the greatest wordsmith, and his language is now littered with Americanisms, but I have no doubt that he was trying to be genuine. In effect, I think he was simply saying, 'I'm here.'

We saw him at that time in Holland with members of the Invictus teams and crowds and it was a complete rerun of how his mother would have operated in similar circumstances. Harry is the joker, the one who wants to be liked, to be part of the crowd and he wants it to be known that, although Royal, he's one of the people, approachable and touchable. He was cycling, chatting, walking around, almost anonymous within the crowd, which is what his mother would have done too. He seemed very much at ease with the protections he received there even in a high-profile role, almost oblivious to his own personal security at some points, which is somewhat at odds with the drama there has been over what he would have wanted, had he and Meghan come back to the UK for a visit. The security risks to him are always going to be the same. Unfortunately, the MPs like Jo Cox and David Amess, who were murdered, did not have the luxury of protection which would hopefully have prevented those incidents from happening, but Harry does have protection which has always been my point. He has a security detail from America; they may not be part of our police, but they are well trained in protecting their client.

As far as the UK is concerned, it was never an option not to give him some assistance to back up the protection he brought with him. I do know he would always have been given a liaison officer – it would not have been in the interests of the British Government to leave him or his family open to any threat. Had he not taken legal action on this point, we wouldn't be discussing this matter but that is a route he chose to take, and he must face the consequences of that in terms of how the public now perceive him. He would have wanted to visit the Queen in any case, and whoever handles his PR would probably have said to him at some point, 'Look, there's no way you can go to the Netherlands without seeing your grandmother and letting the British people know you still care for her in her Jubilee year.' They got that right – the rest of it perhaps needs to be worked on.

Harry doesn't want to be seen as the same sort of man as his brother and father. Instead he wants to be trusted as Diana was. I would say that using that phrase of 'protecting' the Queen was just his language in an umbrella way, and also a sign that he wasn't going to be absent for evermore. He isn't coming back yet but it did leave the door open, and he isn't ruling anything out. No one can actually predict what will happen with Harry, Meghan and their children – anything could happen – but I do think that, at some point in the future, things will change and he will return in some form as an operational prince of the realm. That will please his father certainly, who has made it very clear as to where he sits with trimming down the monarchy and where he wants his sons to be within that. At the moment he's minus one of them but I do think that will change and we'll see Harry back here – but whether Meghan comes too is a different question. There may be a situation, I feel, where he divides his time between two continents, with his wife and children largely staying in the US, where they all seem to feel more comfortable.

At the time of writing, Harry's homecoming doesn't fit with what the Queen wanted when he left. She was understanding towards what he wanted but there was a caveat – *Off you go, have a good time, we love you but I'm afraid you can't be a part of this.* I think that could change because the Royal Family is about to change. Once the Queen goes, and assuming the Prince of Wales becomes King, there are a lot of issues there that will be up for discussion. The subject of Camilla will rise its head for certain as well as looking at exactly how far Charles's wish to trim things will go. How deep does he want it to go? Whether Harry is there or not, he will be playing a part in the background anyway as he is of great media interest even if his popularity rating has dropped. He's still very much part of the scene. I think it will be a very interesting period for the British monarchy.

I feel that the Oprah Winfrey interview with Harry and Meghan was not one that he wanted to happen. I firmly believe that he went along with it at Meghan's insistence, and I had a sense that he was particularly unhappy with that interview. Some of his remarks seemed out of kilter. He seemed unsettled about discussing personal things, particularly about his brother and the alleged racist remark within his family about the likely colour of baby Archie's skin. He has spoken of how it is his turn to be looked after by Diana after she has looked after William, and it begs the question as to why this is something he is remarking upon twenty-five years after her death. It shows just how important she was, and I always saw that he, as the younger of the two, needed his mother a lot more than William, who was much more independent as a boy. Harry was very much the mummy's boy and there is plenty of photographic evidence to show that. While he has never openly spoken about her liaison with Morton's book or the interview with Bashir, the very fact that Harry now finds himself in the midst of major TV interviews would have been something very difficult for him to accept. That's why, in my view, I feel that the Oprah interview would have been more at Meghan's insistence, and resulted in Harry feeling that he had a duty to support her – but perhaps it was a duty with which he felt uncomfortable.

Publishing his own memoir replicates exactly what his mother has done. At the time of the Morton book, had Diana asked me what I thought, I would have said, 'It's not a very good idea, Ma'am.' Actually, that would have been without good reason. Now when people ask me, I understand exactly why she did it and can give very good reasons why it was right for her to do so. Maybe Harry has found himself in the same situation. He's been vilified. He hasn't been ignored, but his side of the story is often one that people did not want to listen to – what better way to get that heard than to write a book? Maybe there is a place for him within his father's idea of a new monarchy, who knows? But maybe it is more relevant for him for now to take a similar route to Diana, to get his story out there in his own words and to continue to engage with people.

Considering Harry said that Diana had done all she could for William and that it was now his turn, this indicates that he does turn these things over in his mind. He still clearly thinks about how she did, and how she still could, help him. His comments seem to suggest that he ponders upon where he sat within the mother-brother-son relationship. I always remember an incident on a journey to Highgrove many years ago when Harry must have been about five, and William seven. They were arguing in the back with Nanny Olga Powell refereeing the weekend argument where they spatted over the usual things which make up sibling annoyances. Eventually, she managed to settle them down. William always wanted the last word, but on this occasion, it fell to Harry. He leaned across and said to his brother, 'It's all right for you – you'll be King one day, but I won't. I can do what I want.'

Diana looked at me and said, 'Where the hell did he get that from?'

I had no idea, but Harry clearly knew these things – things which had been said in his company or which he had overheard being discussed. Even as a five-year-old, he knew exactly the direction of William's life. He was always being groomed for that position and Harry always felt that made him rather more important simply because of who he was. That's not to say he was treated differently in terms of love or possessions or outings – Diana most certainly didn't do that – but mentally, he knew exactly what position he held. Diana was very fair in the way she treated both of her sons, but maybe Harry now feels indeed that it's his turn.

If Diana were alive today, what would her role be? There is no doubt in my mind that she would completely understand the position Harry finds himself in and would probably have been jetting across the Atlantic on a regular basis to offer help. He may very well be happy in LaLaLand, but I believe he is marooned and thinking about his options. I don't think we should rule out any possibility of him returning and this is where Diana would have played a role. She opted out, but if she had lived, I am sure she would have been in a very high-profile role in the charity world, she wouldn't have faded away, and I am also sure she would have supported all of the causes which Harry fights for. I think that may have been his point – his mother would have been very much on his side.

Charles has never known any other life than the one he has, whereas Harry now has a different experience, which began with

Diana. Only they can change it. I think what Charles wants is to remove the more remote members of the family. For all the good work the Kents and Gloucesters have done, he wants it to be him, his sons and perhaps his sister. For him, there has to be a way of coming closer to the public in the way Diana did and I feel that perhaps that still haunts him. Charles always had a problem with that aspect of Diana's personality and the public love for her and it won't disappear at this stage of his life; he won't suddenly understand the approach she had and adopt it himself. They didn't know how to do what she was doing. Harry does. He knows exactly what to do – and that is to be himself, to be normal, and that is what endears him to the public and makes him popular. William's not as good at it as Harry, he's more aligned to his father, who is the one who wants to make the Royals more approachable ironically.

The European approach is completely different. There, the public don't seem to feel the need to doff their caps or curtsey. I once looked after the Queen of Denmark and was staggered by her attitude. I was sent to Greenwich to meet her on her own yacht. I was sure I'd be in the hull, never spoken to again, but in perfect English, she said to me, 'Do come and join us for lunch, have a nice beer and a sandwich.'

'Hang on,' I thought, 'are you speaking to me?'

Yes, she was. I sat there with her and the captain of the ship and had a delightful time up the Thames as if that was quite normal. That would never happen with Charles, and there's the difference. If we want to become part of that European way, there have to be major changes. Harry is arguably someone who could help to do that because of his attitude and because of the way he interacts with the public. The Prince of Wales has a problem in that regard, William less so thanks to Diana, but Harry is the one who can do it.

William recently mentioned that his favourite song was 'The Best' by Tina Turner and I recall that very well. I remember vividly singing it in the car on the way to Highgrove after we had been to see Tina Turner in concert. Diana loved that and made sure we all sang it on every trip for quite some time. She was always creating a sort of party atmosphere and I'm very glad that William remembers that.

I do believe that Harry's move to America via Canada wasn't something he had planned, I don't think that's how he thought it would play out. It was all to do with the way he felt Meghan had been treated by his family since their marriage and he made that choice. He could have just done what they said as that's how it had always been, or he could do what he thought was right. I used to hear Charles say, 'I can't do anything – they tell me what to do, I can't do anything myself.' They were trapped and that's what Harry reacted against – he got out. He knows he'll always be a Prince of the Realm – no one can take that away from him – but I think it was his love and concern for Meghan which made him make that change. He had seen himself as an operational member of the Firm, as a young, likeable prince who knew that he had a global status, but he was prepared to give that away in order to protect his wife.

Very few people have gone across the drawbridge and shut the portcullis to see how they operate. It isn't just one big happy family where everyone chats and has a good time. When the circus stops, they live a life of days gone by. That wasn't something that Meghan was ever going to enjoy. Once the wedding service was over, everyone went back to type – they all get shunted back to their part of the castle and you're on your own. It must have been very difficult for Meghan and I don't think they made her very welcome. When you look at the footage of the Prince of Wales and the Duchess when the vicar's sermon seemed to have no end, when his time at the lectern had run well over his permitted royal slot, their reaction seems unkind. Bishop Michael Curry was doing his bit to try to bring some normality into the institution. Even the Queen had welcomed him and the gospel choir, to make the occasion feel a little more like home for Meghan, but the Royals didn't particularly like it. This was the chapel that Henry VIII used to worship in – they now had to face someone coming from across the Atlantic and making changes to an institution they believed was working perfectly well.

There is always an underlying issue of intrigue with Diana, and certainly the Bashir interview was a remarkable period in her life. I thought I knew about it, but I am finding out even more through speaking about it all in this book and with all of the recent revelations. I've never stopped thinking about these things as I'm still talking about it. From 1993, there was a change in her attitude – notably towards me as part of her security, which she was rather suspicious about. The closing stages of her life are interesting.

I've been inside the box of magic tricks with royalty and seen it all. Diana wasn't perfect, none of us are, but I could see the difficulties that faced her given who she was, and it needn't have been that way. To have survived for the period she did was extraordinary – I never thought she would last as long as that. I couldn't see it, somebody in a marriage that wasn't working – there must come a point when you either say to yourself, I'm going to live with this as it is – in which case it'll be fine – or I'm going to have to do something about it. Diana couldn't live with it, that was certain, so it was a question of how long she would live with it as it was.

The fact that she has left such a legacy for her sons, and in the form they have taken, may not be so surprising given that mothers always leave something behind for their children in one way or another, but that changes entirely when you add royalty into the mix. William and Harry are very much their mother's boys in so many ways, even though there are differences between them. Although William has perhaps reverted more to a world away from the limelight when it comes to putting his children in the public eye, he does try to engage, he does try to bring a more modernised approach. But with Harry, we can see Diana more – and when he returns, which I think he will do, I believe that will be even clearer.

CHAPTER 24

ROS COWARD

'She's watching over us.'

IT IS VERY HARD to predict whether or not there will be a space for Prince Harry to come back into the royal fold. I do think it is often represented in the press that he and Meghan flounced off to California, set up their Netflix deal and were more focused on money than anything else. To me, it always seemed more as if the door had been slammed in his face, and that he wasn't really given much option in terms of what he could do. I think the security issue was always a genuine one for the couple, because staying in the UK with the level of real media exploitation of them was unbearable. They sell well, and they are excellent clickbait through the media constantly stirring up stories about them. If I were them, I would be extraordinarily worried about coming back to the UK because I feel that the situation is somewhat febrile. There is a lot of hatred that can get stirred up, so I understand why they thought they couldn't stay around, but also why they felt excluded – somehow half in and half out of the Royal Family.

Even though Charles is likely to be the next King, I believe that there is still a strong groundswell of feeling that William should be next, even if there are no constitutional grounds for that to happen. There is a popular feeling for such a change, as well as a popular liking of Harry. Contrary to what the press thinks, I feel that people would be very pleased if the younger prince found some way of coming back into the fold. It seems to me that the response to him on social media and in newspaper comments appears to be much more supportive than the tabloid coverage, especially from some of the more obsessed commentators such as Piers Morgan. Additionally, a lot of women greatly like and admire Meghan, despite what the tabloids might have us think. She might be a bit too 'Californian' for some tastes, but the tabloid negativity is extreme. For many people, Meghan is a glamorous, interesting, iconic figure, rather than how she is represented by the tabloids en masse. They are running with a particular narrative about the couple and anything they do is interpreted in the most unfavourable possible of lights. This negative narrative makes it very difficult for the Sussexes ever to be seen as doing anything 'right'.

Harry is the one whom people regard as carrying Diana's flame. He doesn't want to be thought of as removed from the people or too grand, and his recent comments about its being 'time' for Diana to help him tend to suggest that he is going through a period of reflection. He has said:

'It is almost as though she's done her bit with my brother and now she's very much, like, helping me. Got him set up.

And now she's helping me set up. That's what it feels like, you know? He's got his kids. I've got my kids, you know, the circumstances are obviously different. But now, I feel her presence in almost everything that I do now. But definitely more so in the last two years than ever before. Without question. So, she's watching over us.'

People undoubtedly do relate to Harry in the same way as they did to Diana, if not to the same extent. And the fact that he called his daughter Lilibet suggests his love for and commitment to his grandmother, the Queen. During the Oprah Winfrey interview a sadness came over him regarding his separation from the Queen and from his wider family. His body language suggested that he was uncomfortable in his present position and being so isolated from his family. He is in a very difficult position. We don't hear both sides of the story, but it doesn't seem as if the Royal Family are going out of their way to reach out – they could visit, they could go to see Harry's children, they have the security to do these things, but it would appear that they choose not to. He is isolated from them and therefore dependent on Meghan, which might mean that he goes along with her wishes on so many matters, including that interview.

There is a curious repetition, on so many levels, in Harry's life, as compared with Diana's: the sense of being an outsider, of having to make his own way and his own decisions, the lack of ease he finds in life, the extent to which both of them tried to get their voices over in interviews. Here he is, doing so much that is the same.

Harry's comment that William has had Diana's support and

now it's his turn suggests he thinks that, so far, William has had all the luck. Not from jealousy, but because the older prince's position is secure and things are going well for him. Harry was almost implying, *It's time for me to have a bit of that.* There must be so much internal conflict about not being with his family and the manner in which that happened, the split with his brother, the hostility of some of the British press… Harry wasn't brought up to lead an ordinary life but he seems to be making a good stab at it. Looking at him with his children, you can see he is happy in his role as a father and has suddenly been able to live in a more relaxed way. There are negatives and positives to his life, and that can be an uncomfortable place, feeling you've alienated yourself or been alienated from people you care about, people whose approval you would like, but actually feeling quite badly treated by them. Harry's comment during the Oprah interview that his father and brother are 'trapped' within the system and that he feels compassion for that suggests a struggle and a journey, a realisation that while his family have trapped him they are themselves trapped.

The British monarchy still has a very long way to go before it can be anything like other European royals. What does Charles mean when he says it needs to be modernised and slimmed down? Does he mean he won't have anyone to squeeze his toothpaste any more or is he going to dispense with all the pomp and ceremony?

Although William is more in touch with the people than his father was at the same age, and is clearly a much more approachable figure, nevertheless when we look at the styling of his children, he is still stuck in the past. George at only eight years old still has his little tie on, his hair brushed immaculately and a very serious expression. The children have a Norland nanny, sometimes dressed in her Mary Poppins hat and brown, starched uniform, something Diana would never have had. It's as if they've gone back in time. I'm sure that Harry's children will be much more relaxed and won't be brought up, even in part, by people wearing uniforms.

Often in the accounts of Diana, her quest for privacy can be a bone of contention. Depending on people's perspectives, she is sometimes ridiculed for the lengths she went to, going out with a wig to disguise herself, tipping a baseball cap down low over her face or wearing clothes which no one would associate with a princess. She went on the Tube with her sons, she took them to fast-food outlets, she wanted them to do things other children did with their parents, and this was something Charles could never fathom. Why in the world would they do that when they had cars to take them everywhere? It is perhaps hard to see how someone with an attitude like that can modernise the monarchy.

Harry probably didn't intend to give up his life in Britain; I think he got plunged into a situation where moving to North America was the only way forward. When the relationship with Meghan became public – and it was quite early on – Harry very quickly made a statement asking the press to stop what he perceived to be their racist coverage of her. He was protective of her from the very beginning. He had fallen passionately in love; had that somehow triggered anxiety, given how his mother had been treated?

For her part, Meghan would have found the restrictions not just difficult but also incomprehensible. For the Royals themselves, their duty is their life and tradition seems to shape their days, but for her, it would have been a sort of madness. I think she was trying to say that in the Oprah interview, that she just didn't 'get it'. When Meghan said that she hadn't really known much about royalty before meeting Harry, many people scoffed. 'Everyone knows about the British royalty,' they said. What she probably meant was that she didn't know about the palaver around it.

But it is not Meghan who is repeating the Diana journey. It's Harry. He's the one who has found himself on the outside, who has been ostracised and is left trying to make a meaningful life for himself, trying to negotiate privacy for his family outside of the royal world. His Oprah Winfrey interview could almost be seen as a version of Diana's Bashir interview – simultaneously an event which would definitely not heal any wounds, and something he felt compelled to do to allow his wife's voice to be heard. At so many levels there is repetition. Harry has become alienated from his own family. A great deal of what should be private has become media fodder with, for instance, press stories involving Meghan's father and half-sister. He has been cut adrift with his family seemingly making little effort to heal the wounds, something that is likely to be hugely painful to him.

Diana always wanted a role, she always wanted guidance and recognition from the Royal Family and to be given some support. But she wanted to do things differently, her own way – and that was never going to happen, given the deep-rooted traditionalism and emotional limitations of the Royal Family. Looking at Harry, it seems that the Royal Family have learned very little emotional literacy at all from Diana – which is a terrible shame.

CHAPTER 25

KEN WHARFE

'If you find someone you love in your life,
then hang on to that love.'

I THINK DIANA WOULD have been shocked and surprised by the outpouring of public grief when she died, as she was now on a course of action which was a new role for her and was unlikely to be thinking of herself as the 'old' Diana who was still in people's minds. She had gone – she would think she wasn't part of that anymore. The interest was now in her and Dodi, some in the landmines campaign in Angola and Mozambique, but she would believe her future would be rather more normal. The grief came as a shock to everybody. I never thought for one moment it would be like that.

I remember being at Kensington Palace soon after, and people were walking towards the Palace in their hundreds, all carrying flowers. Within a short period of time, there was a mass of flowers within the Gardens, at Buckingham Palace, and at Balmoral. People identified with Diana – that level of grief never happened when the Queen Mother died a few years later, for example. I don't think one single carnation was laid anywhere when she died. The circumstances added to that – no one could ever have believed Diana would die in such a way. When her brother got involved in such a way at the funeral, it was a lightning attack on both the Royal Family and the media. I was outside Westminster Abbey that day and I have never seen so many people in the streets of London in my entire policing career, nor could I ever have imagined that the response to Spencer's speech would be like a wave crashing over the Abbey. It was an extraordinary moment. I've often thought, *Why?* What magic did this woman have to gather hundreds of thousands of people in one city alone and to make them feel that way?

I bumped into Richard Kay of the *Daily Mail* that day, in the press pen outside the Abbey, and he was in tears. Everybody was weeping from what I can remember, even those hardened journalists. And yet there was a coach of her close friends who arrived for her funeral. I knew most of them and they looked as if they were on a day out or going to a party. Yes, they were sad, but they weren't in tears like people in the street who had never met her. They were there to honour their friend, but even they couldn't really work out the level of upset.

We have to acknowledge that something changed. The out-pouring of grief from people who had never met her was formed from what they had read or seen in the media. For the first time they felt they could identify with someone like her. There was an affinity with this woman from people who had never met her. I can understand that. When you meet the Queen or Prince Charles for the first time, you are nervous; no matter whether you're a royalist or republican, you're starstruck. Diana had the complete opposite effect. You felt she was a friend, you felt that you knew her. She integrated with and reacted to the people in the street. No matter which country she was in, she was always the same.

I don't think I personally grieved for Diana when she died – I was shocked more than anything else. I'd moved on anyway and I was certainly sad that her life had been cut short, but my biggest memory is of shock when I received the call to say she was dead. I could have understood if she had been attacked or shot, although there weren't that many fixated individuals who would have done that anyway – we're in different times now and I think she may have been in more danger and a possible target for terrorists or stalkers. At that time, I was upset but I felt no guilt. She was a good friend although there is a terminology one is very careful to use when working with Royals. Before I worked with her, I went to many classes and modules which gave some background about such positions, and indeed warnings saying they would never become your friend, and that you were there to serve the Commissioner. I remember speaking to Diana's bodyguard at the time, Graham Smith who said, 'Whatever you heard in those briefings, Ken, I wouldn't worry about it. This woman is so totally different to the rest of the Royal Family – that isn't to suggest she will become your friend as such, but there is a friendly, albeit professional, relationship with her.' That was simply her style – you couldn't fight against it, because if you did, she wouldn't want you there and you'd have to move on. So, I did feel that I'd lost a professional friend in that sense.

I remember meeting soon after her death with colleagues who had worked with her, and we chatted about her death and the accident. All of us certainly felt this would have been nothing other than an accident. We reflected and reminisced but none of us got our handkerchiefs out and sobbed our way home. I was sad about a young woman and mother dying but I never anticipated this would happen – or that twenty-five years later, we'd still be talking about it. I thought we'd have moved on.

Why do we still care? When I wrote my first book in 2002, it was in reaction to the sea change which had come about with the introduction of Camilla into the public sphere. She was given a PR guru to make it all look good and I was thinking, 'Hang on, this is really crazy. No one ever believed Diana and writing her off isn't fair.' Even then, there were about eighty books written about Diana and only two of their authors had known her – one of them being me!

Younger people want to know who she was and what her magic was. Many of them weren't even alive when she was around – whereas to me, I can hardly believe it has been that long. I don't think we'll be talking about the Duke of Edinburgh in twenty-five years the way we're still talking about Diana. She's fixed in time, which aids the near-obsession we still have with her. It's hard for younger people to imagine that people in such high status die in a car crash, which adds to many of them not believing it could have been as simple. So much has been said and printed and continues to be any time William or Harry are mentioned. They are the future of the monarchy, and she is always in their story.

Diana made people feel important – they were never cast away. I went on to work for the Duke of Kent and it was extremely professionally satisfying with no complications. His interactions with the public were very sterile. I recall journeying all the way down the Eastern China seaboard, to Japan, to South Africa, on many incredible journeys, but it was just him and me. No one was interested, there was no media at all. He is a man who has done incredible work as a true loyal supporter of the Queen, carrying out extraordinary work across the world. When I went to him, he said, 'I don't know why you're here – nobody knows who I am. They know who you are, though, don't they?' Even he couldn't understand it. Why did they turn up for Diana opening a church fête, but not when he toured South Africa? He was right, very few people were interested.

With Diana, it was the opposite with all its attendant problems. We are still dissecting her form of magic which ended simply because she pulled out of the scene that was her life, because of the state of her own marriage.

I am still inundated with requests for interviews about Diana, from America, France, Holland, Australia, Japan ... Everyone still wants to know about her. They want to know, what was the appeal? That is the main story, and the answer always is that they liked her style and approach, they liked the way she actively enjoyed being with people, they want to know about Camilla and Charles, they want to know the essence of Diana.

William and Harry are not stupid, and Harry will say what he wants to say even more so than William. As children, they would have been aware of Camilla and of James Hewitt – but they would just have thought of them as Mummy and Daddy's friends. As you get older, you look back at childhood and see things through a different lens. That will be no different for William and Harry – they will recall events and moments that now have a bigger impact, that they can see for what they were, especially where Camilla was involved. The heartache which has come out since then regarding where Camilla sat within all of that will be something for them to dissect. William is probably more capable of saying, *It's not my life now, we have to move on.* In Harry's case, I think he has found it more difficult. I remember when the photographs came out soon after Diana's death and it became clear that Charles and Camilla were to become an official item – that must have been very hard for them both, but I feel it would have hit Harry more. They have no doubt both looked back and asked, *What role did this woman play in my parents' marriage? It must have been difficult for Mummy.* We know what happened, we just don't know how much it affected them both.

Harry talks passionately about the media as far as his mother is concerned and that is understandable, especially in the way he relates it all to Meghan. He is rather overprotective of Diana in that respect, as he must now know that, in the latter part of her life in particular, she did liaise and negotiate with certain sections of the media. I think his wish to speak publicly is deeper, it is the way Diana and Meghan have been dealt with by members of the Royal Family, the lack of support his wife received, in the same way as Diana was never given approval or support for what she did. With both women, he will be aware of how quickly things turned back to normal after marriage and suddenly both were holed up in the Royal Estate with an expectation that they would simply follow rules rather than forge their own path. As with Diana, they wanted Meghan and Harry to go away, get on with their lives, and cause no bother. I can't say what Meghan wanted out of all this, but Harry was a very popular prince at the time and part of the future of the monarchy as he was charismatic in the eyes of the British public. I'm not so certain Meghan knew what she was getting into – they would not have wanted her to make a stand just as they hadn't wanted Diana to make a stand.

People do ask me if Harry will be back and the answer is: I don't know but I think so. His public comments would no doubt never air or be published if he was still in his role in the UK, but he has his own storyline now. If he ever criticises the monarchy and his father, it will be hard for him to return. Diana would have been crucial for his guidance by virtue of her own experience. That aspect will never go away.

Twenty-five years ago, Diana was laying the grounds for the changes we do see. The Queen has been on a Zoom meeting with fellow Covid patients. Angela Kelly, her longstanding right-hand maid/confidante, has been given permission to write a book. She did things that had never been done before, and it is only now that they can see what she knew was right. It is the people who will decide whether the monarchy continues, and the monarchy itself needs to accept that. The Royal Family is much more open than it ever was, and Diana saw that was the way to go many years ago.

She always felt that the power of her husband's court was far more powerful than hers because of the division. Initially, she was part of the Prince and Princess of Wales's Office, which was effectively his office with his wife being part of it as well. In the early days, Diana was raising two boys, so her public involvement was fairly minimal. The star player was the Prince; he was the one going around the country and going abroad. As Diana moved through parenthood and was able to get out more, she started to become more involved and take up more of his office space in terms of female assistants, sharing the accountant and suchlike. She would go into the office and have a cup of tea with them, which the Prince couldn't understand at all – he was too old school to go and mix with the below-stairs staff.

When she changed tack and started to get involved in higher-profile public engagements that required more, her office began to grow. She didn't have the power he had, she didn't have the links with the men in grey suits, the secretaries and private secretaries to the Queen and so forth. Diana always felt she didn't have the power in her staff to fight her corner. These men in grey suits were powerful as they had links to both the monarch and the Government.

The classic grey suit to me was Nicholas Soames. He was a member of the Conservative Government and as a friend of the Prince of Wales was duty-bound out of loyalty to protect him at whatever cost. He went on national television to say that Diana was paranoid and that triggered other people to come out of the woodwork and say exactly the same thing. That was Diana's problem – how could she compete with them? Who would stand up in defence of her? Once there would clearly be no more children and her role changed when she worked with controversial patronages, she got so much more publicity and controversy.

As we look back, twenty-five years after the death of Diana, I honestly believe we can say she changed the monarchy – certainly while she was there, and now in the lives of her sons, particularly Harry. Whether the Royal Family has ever engaged in such similar levels of reflection I cannot say, but if they have, I hope they realise just what a remarkable young woman they had in their midst. If they could find it in themselves to also reflect on the many times they failed her, then I think that could actually benefit them as we – hopefully – move towards a time for modernisation of the monarchy.

Diana was, despite everything she went through, a woman who believed in love. As she famously said, 'If you find someone you love in your life, then hang on to that love.' I like to think she is often remembered with love, and I like to think that history will look on her with kindness.

APPENDIX

Selected letters from Ken Wharfe's collection

Dear Ken

I like you very much but you cannot sing very well.

Love
Putt Putt
Ding Ding

from Harry

Personal

K. Wharfe, Esq.,
C/o H.R.H. The Princess of Wales' Office
St. James's Palace
London S.W.1.

ARDENCAPLE
ISLE OF SEIL
BY OBAN
ARGYLL PA34 4TN

30/5/90

My dear Ken,
well, how was Italy?
Longing to hear & do hope
all looks set fair for the
trip - a lovely beacon to look
forward to.
I'm v. chuffed with my
Super gran badge - and lots
of thanks and Brownie points
for finding such a gem.
I wrote with suggested
dates to Graham (the roster
fixer?) for a visit here - to
date not a squeak so how

persistent premonition of a
stroke or something of that
ilk & being still married I would.
I feel have always some
responsibility, so keen to be free.
Must stop & catch the post
With love,
Frances.

14/6/90

Dear Ken,
The prospect of you three
merry men solo-venting to
Ardencaple in August is quite
something to look forward to...!!
Anyway just to say apart
from Verona have anything onits
or rather anytime - If suitable
would any of you like to
hitch north with me on return
from there?? No hurry to know
and I do realise now that all
3 of you are remarkably
coy about writing letters...!
Sad that the last 24 hours
have been hurtful - My mother
is a jealous, interfering old

261

ACKNOWLEDGEMENTS

W̲e would like to thank Linda Watson Brown for her sensitive and sterling work. She was a pleasure to work with, and her cheerfulness kept us going as Covid struck us down one after another.